Ecological Enlightenment

ECOLOGICAL ENLIGHTENMENT

Essays on the Politics of the Risk Society

Ulrich Beck

Translated by Mark A. Ritter

HUMANITIES PRESS

NEW JERSEY

Originally published as *Politik in der Risikogesellschaft,*
©Suhrkamp Verlag Frankfurt am Main 1991.

This translation first published 1995 by Humanities Press
International, Inc., Atlantic Highlands, New Jersey 07716.

English translation ©1995 by Humanities Press International, Inc.
Chapter 4, "The Anthropological Shock: Chernobyl and the Contours
of Risk Society," translated by John Torpey, first
published in *Berkeley Journal of Sociology: A Critical Review*
32 (1987): 153–65; ©1987.

Library of Congress Cataloging-in-Publication Data

Beck, Ulrich, 1944–
    [Politik in der Risikogesellschaft. English]
    Ecological enlightenment : essays on the politics of the risk
society / Ulrich Beck ; translated by Mark A. Ritter.
        p. cm.
    Includes bibliographical references and index.
    ISBN 0–391–03831–1 (cloth)—ISBN 0–391–03832–X (paper)
    1. Risk—Sociological aspects. 2. Progress. 3. Industry—
Environmental aspects. 4. Technology—Social aspects.
5. Environmental degradation. I. Title.
HM201.B3813   1994
303.44—dc20   93–1682
                                              CIP

A catalog record for this book is available from the British
Library

Printed in the United States of America

10 9 8 7 6 5 4 3 2

Contents

1

Politics in Risk Society

The successes of the ecological movement force us all to keep repeating ourselves. It has become a given in contemporary consciousness that species are dying out, that oceans are being contaminated, that climatic catastrophe is looming—these basic assumptions are shared by the Communists and the conservatives, by the chemical industry and fundamentalist Greens. But, not only is any action to address these problems blocked, there has not even been any discussion of what it is that prevents action, or how to overcome it. That is the objective of this inquiry into politics in risk society.

When I was experimenting with the concept of a "risk society" in 1984, it was a test-tube product from my desk and aroused general skepticism. Since then, the term has entered the general discourse, and many people use it as if they know what it means. Yet there is still something prickly about it. It takes a certain amount of guts to call Germany, the home of the economic miracle, a risk society. Supporters of the Christian Democratic Union (the CDU) courageously add "our" when they say it, probably meaning "this risk society of ours." I am rarely criticized anymore for inventing the term; indeed, I am now often accused of having shaped someone else's concept to fit the market, which is a beautiful example of why sociologists can only circulate nonpatented inventions. Being taken for granted is the highest practical success to which sociologists can aspire.

The debate has stirred up a lot of controversy. Some find the concept of risk society too tame, too actuarial, too closely attached to the monumental error it seeks to combat, too German in its prosperous pessimism: "We've had the lobster, now please pass the disaster!" But didn't I struggle for practical opportunities and perspectives? "That's just the problem," others object, and reproach me for being a Social

1

Democrat! Many of the objections rage against the grim reality that makes this concept seem self-evident. Well-meaning friends hope to deter me from similar neologisms in the future, because they suspect a causal relation between my linguistic inventiveness and the events illustrating them. But now to the point.

I

"Risk society" means an epoch in which the dark sides of progress increasingly come to dominate social debate. What no one saw and no one wanted—self-endangerment and the devastation of nature—is becoming the motive force of history. Here we are not concerned with analyzing hazards but with proving that new opportunities for arranging society arise under the pressure of the industrial threat that humanity will annihilate itself and the breakup of social classes and social contrasts that it causes.

Central to the political analysis is the *distinction between risks and threats.* What marks a watershed, in my view, is society's confrontation with the possibility of artificially produced self-annihilation. Unlike the risks of early industrial society, contemporary nuclear, chemical, ecological, and biological threats are (1) not limitable, either socially or temporally; (2) not accountable according to the prevailing rules of causality, guilt, and liability; and (3) neither compensable nor insurable. Where private insurance companies deny their protection—as in large chemical plants—the boundary between calculable risks and incalculable threats is violated again and again. To use an analogy, the regulating system for the "rational" control of industrial devastation is about as effective as a bicycle brake on a jetliner.

The transformation of the unseen side effects of industrial production into global flash points is not an environmental problem but a flagrant institutional crisis of industrial society, with considerable political content. Threats are produced industrially, externalized economically, individualized juridically, legitimized scientifically, and minimized politically.[1] The key question is, How can a policy of ecological self-limitation, by contrast, gain power and enforceability?

II

Let the reader be warned against three types of naiveté. First, a policy of self-limitation can rely neither on the size of the threat nor on the universality of the victimization. Many threats, the prime example being nuclear radiation, are invisible and are hard to identify in everyday life, which means that devastation and protest are *symbolically medi-ated* ("forest destruction," for example). Given that many threats lack any sensory character, the only way that culturally blinded daily life can become "sighted" is through culturally meaningful and publicly exhibited images and symbols.

Second, the *resistance* to insight into the threat grows with the size and proximity of the threat. The people most severely affected are often precisely the ones who deny the threat most vehemently, and they *must* deny it in order to keep on living. Bombardment with apoca-lyptic visions can therefore easily seem to be counterproductive and to strengthen the sense of powerlessness and fatalism.

Third, the new social movements are no likelier to discover the Marxian "revolutionary subject" in risk society than were the traditional leftist movements in class society.

So, there is no "ecological proletariat." Is that the end of the mat-ter? Not in my assessment, since this ignores a new mobilization to action: that alarming of the system that will occur as people become aware of the general threats to life in the milieu of bureaucratically administered security. This is the *"political reflexivity"* of threat. Once citizens realize that the guardians of rationality and order also legalize threats to survival, then all hell breaks loose politically. The search for the political subject in industrial and class society corresponds to the search for political reflexivity in risk society. *Political reflexivity* may be an echo effect, depending on collective attention, on the sounding board of the safety-oriented control institutions and the mass media, and limited therefore to the special conditions of developed wealthy democracies. *Political reflexivity* also serves both the ecological protest and an expansive industrial policy. The fact that public opinion polls now rank ecology as "most urgent" is due to a great deal of activity from below, but also to this irritating political quality of both normalized *and* advancing threats of annihilation. How should that be understood?

III

What was at stake in the old industrial conflict of labor against capital were positives: profits, prosperity, consumer goods. In the new eco-logical conflict, on the other hand, what is at stake are negatives: losses, devastation, threats. The ecological conflict, to use Claus Offe's no-tion, is a *negative-sum game of collective self-damage.*[2] At first glance, then, this is a game between losers, more precisely, losers who either refuse to admit their loss or who choose to blame it on others. It is an end-game, if you will (in Beckett's sense as well), in which the advantages struggled for are always relative and always threatened, and which at heart consists in either denying (whitewashing, minimizing) the threats or, to the extent that denial fails, preventing or concealing any specific attribution or general accountability.

By contrast, the survival interest asserts the highly legitimate general claims of preserving life and averting all the looming threats. The new and dominant fact is thus the negative conflict, the distribution of loss. It is shadow boxing; directly at stake are only disadvantages and indirect advantages: cost avoidance, corporate image, market position, and values such as health, recreation, and contact with nature. The central point, however, is the shifting of consequences, the definition of consequences, and the accountability for consequences. The longer the shadows of progress grow, the more the industrial perpetrators tend to lose their own shadow. They end up as purely abstract creatures, concrete only in the radioactivity or toxicity they cause.

No one wins the ecological game of roulette; there are no victories, only relative, transitory advantages, which are always threatened, first by the progressive devastation that slips under the boundary between perpetrators and victims and then by the always provisional victories in the contest to deny threats and shift blame. These advantages may be suddenly overturned by new scientific knowledge or by the needling of small groups. Threat positions are powder kegs, which in some cases can be exploded by a single spark of information. They imply a wholesale uncertainty for everyone, including the power centers from industry to politics. I am told that the directors of global corporations are spellbound as they watch small groups in the North Sea islands, for instance, declare a "chemical-free zone." They know or suspect that such activities could set off a firestorm in which all their marketing and safety designs would be swept away without being able to exercise any effective opposition. Even the expressed interest in a "unionization" of the ecological movement points to industrial power's helpless realization of its own impotence in the face of the diffuseness, unpredictability, and *high legitimacy* of ecological protest.

IV

In the conflict of capital versus labor, wage reductions are reflected on the balance sheet as increases in profit. In contrast, in the ecological conflict, where what are at stake are negatives, there is no direct intermeshing of opposing interests. Shifting blame for threats or denying that threats exist does not imply any skimming off of profits. What does happen is the *marginalization of the injured parties*. If the injury cannot be denied, then it must remain as diffuse and unpredictable as possible, and it must be concentrated in delimited enclaves of damage. This will probably not work, or it will work only temporarily, because the devastation is universal and the populace is becoming more ecologically sensitive. The influential middle classes are increasingly affected by the damage, and the prosperity they have worked for (their yards, their houses, their vacations) is threatened. It is a rule of thumb in sociology that alarm bells go off in the political system when the social middle suffers. Another intensifying factor is that even the children of the decision makers in business, technology, and politics ask probing questions. None of this, however, implies that ecological awareness advances automatically.

V

Two stages in the ecological conflict must be distinguished. The first is a general struggle to uncover the threats, because the first thing everyone sees is the opportunity for industrial expansion. The threat and its dimensions must be exposed despite the illusions of faith in progress. Quite surprisingly, the ecological movement emerged victorious from this conflict (which in Germany started in the 1970s). For instance, German citizens are now more concerned about the ecological issue than about unemployment. These successes have come from a policy of presenting realistic horror scenarios based on scientific diagnosis, which has revealed the latent scandalousness of conditions, even measured according to the system's own claims. These scenarios triggered the political reflexivity in the mass media, and the news penetrated into all niches and strata of society.

A second stage results when knowledge of the dimensions of the devastation has been accepted in principle, but there is still no action, or at best only cosmetic action, taken. Perhaps the representatives of industry have learned from the citizens' groups (for instance, by dramatizing the hole in the ozone layer, they bring nuclear energy back into the game); perhaps institutional foot-dragging has taken over; or perhaps priorities changed to reflect the themes of the day (for instance, after the lightning rise of West Germany because of the collapse of East Germany, everything that was previously questionable in the West became squeaky clean).

The conflict that then arises is basically an accountability conflict. The plans for shifting blame and the switch-settings for normalization in the institutions become crucial. We have moved increasingly into this stage since the mid-1980s, without quite realizing it. Not the least important reason for the stagnation of the ecological movement is the fact that its topics and issues have become established: all political groups have inscribed them on their banners. The first phase's audacious piercing of the armor of denial cannot win any new prizes.

In any case, that attitude cannot pin down and open up the main problem, which is the legally sanctioned poisoning that occurs because acceptable levels of toxicity are not established or are set too high, and because the affected parties cannot produce sufficiently "rigorous" proofs of causality. Protest gets stuck in what was once the essential basis for its victory: scientific horror scenarios that remain blind and that immobilize people in the face of normal institutional and political procedures.

The general tendency to cover up must be freed from individual cases and related to the historical flaws in the regulatory system, so that alternative regulations can enable and implement different distributions of cost, different manners, different obligations for justification, and different public learning processes. Even small, seemingly unspectacular steps (in liability law, for instance) could have major effects, because they operate on a large scale and over a long term and, if politically successful, can make exemplary progress possible.

Turned a different way, this means that it is necessary to create accountability on all levels and using all means. This implies, for instance:

- changing the burden of proof, so that the representatives of industry and the sciences must justify themselves in public (the environmental laws in California take this first step);
- opening committees and expert groups in the gray zone of politics, science, and industry to a variety of disciplines, to alternative experts, and to laypeople;
- raising liability issues and reforming liability law;
- revealing the lack of insurance or the uninsurability of many technological mega-projects;
- reformulating the polluter-pays principle by creating regional accountability between harmed and benefited business sectors, such as coastal regions, with their hotels and restaurants, and the chemical/industrial regions that create the pollutants that drive away tourists;
- suggesting and negotiating agreements that recognize damage and establish compensation payments between industrial plants in a region and its population (as is sometimes done in Japan).

There are many starting points. For example, acceptable levels could initially be set very high, to be corrected downward only under the burden of difficult-to-obtain evidence, or, considering the general groping in the fog here, the safety of the public could be given precedence over the user interests of industry. Why can outdoor experiments (as well as many normal types of chemical and other mega-technical production) be conducted without insurance protection? How is it possible that, even though the Genetic Technology Law talks of "no-fault threat insurance," in the end the burden of proof is once again placed on the victims? (This means that the losses and devastation are shifted onto the victims almost a priori.) Polarizations in the ecological conflict may be diffuse, but the possibility of regional crises grows alongside the threats and their visibility. Would it not be possible, for example, to identify victim and polluter sectors on a regional and national level and make the latter pay up? And the same for polluter countries and those that must absorb the pollution? This would break the anonymity and create an instructive conflict, which would expose the failure of the established accountability standards. Examples include—but are obviously not limited to—the Italian industrial centers from the Po northward and the resort towns on the Adriatic, and the conflicts between the industrial regions on the Rhine and inhabitants of the North Sea coast.

Like the "social question" in the nineteenth century, the "ecological question" today must be related to social (that is, institutional) opportunities for action that fit the context in which the question arises. There was no unambiguous answer to the question of causality for factory or occupational accidents in the nineteenth century. Did the worker cause the accident himself by mistakenly sticking his now-cut-off arm into the machine? Did the engineer who designed the machinery cause the accident? Perhaps it was the entrepreneur, who was turning the screw for higher production? Causality always remains ambiguous, for philosophical and scientific reasons. The causality problem had to be, and even in the social area still has to be, settled by agreements (that is, social agreements) worked out through conflict, and legal standards had to be established. These historical experiences must be transferred to the ecological question, and must counteract both a false naturalism and a widespread strident moralism that blind us to the complex modes of handling and repressing ecological issues in the law, science, politics, and so forth.[3]

VI

Industry has learned from the environmental movement. It is not the demonstration of the threat and how it can be eliminated (as was assumed in the first phase) but the race to repress mega-risks that increasingly determines the political backdrop. One need no longer deny a threat; it is just as good to blacken the alternative. One can eliminate a risk by publicizing another one, inflating it and enthroning it as the risk to survival surpassing all others. This happens particularly when several mega-risks are competing for political attention, that is, against the background of a successful information policy. Nuclear energy, for instance, no longer needs to be promoted directly; instead, it can conquer markets "defensively," so to speak, in reaction to depictions of the threat to the ozone layer. The surplus of possibilities for doom permits one to play a game of transpositioning in the public dramatization of risks, a game in which someone else's blacker black can whitewash one's own black.

Doesn't this policy of repressing threats operate with an almost intimidating perfection? Perhaps, but people also fail to understand that it is tantamount to playing with political fire.

After all, the ecological issue, considered politically and sociologically, focuses at heart on a *systematic, legalized violation of fundamental civil rights*—the citizen's right to life and freedom from bodily harm. This violation is not going on incidentally, accidentally, or individually, but in broad daylight, as part of the development of industry, prosperity, and technical rationality, in the glare of the mass media and in an alert democracy of citizens' groups. It is only a slight exaggeration to say that the protectors of the constitution violate their trust when they permit ecologically self-destructive types of production. Even Thomas Hobbes, a theoretician of state and society who was certainly no forerunner of the Frankfurt School and who advocated a strong, authoritarian state, also mentions the individual citizen's right to resist, and in words that sound surprisingly contemporary. If a state produces circumstances that threaten life, so that the citizen "must refrain from food, medicines, air, and whatever else is necessary for the preservation of life," Hobbes argues, "then the citizen is free to resist."[4] In the ecological crisis we are dealing with a breach of fundamental rights that is cushioned and disguised during prosperity but that has socially destabilizing long-term effects that can scarcely be overestimated.

VII

In the first industrial conflict, the stakes were a relatively limited range of political options, such as property issues, co-management in plants, and redistribution. A strange universalism erupted along with the ecological conflict. Everything can be caught in the undertow of this dispute: air, water, energy, industrial products, production processes, standards, agencies, companies, political parties. In the spotlight of the general threat to human life, objective constraints lose both their objectivity and their constraining character, and become flexible and avoidable through alternatives and through other, previously excluded, possibilities and decisions concealed implicitly within themselves.

The interesting thing here is that even the cross-linking between the power institutions is changing. Parties and institutions, not least among them labor unions and co-management rules, developed to balance out the conflicts that grew from poverty. In the ecological conflicts over distributing exposure to undesirable things, the active agents of modernization—management, national and local governments, labor unions, and political parties—suddenly find themselves in situations of dependency, with unforeseen associates and opponents certainly not represented in the system of compromise negotiation. These uncontrollable dependencies can subvert the certainties of that system. In other words, *legal* (contractual) security and *social* (actual) security no longer coincide. The public sphere and those who make it and provide it with news play a decisive role; overnight scientists' new theories and questions can throw out all the plans for shifting threats, as, it goes without saying, can the citizens' and consumer organizations; nor can we forget Old Father Accident, who may appear on the other side of the world or among one's competition and cause one's own plans for security to collapse in the floodlight of an alarmed public.

Ecological conflicts have a moral and social deep structure that results from the violation of survival norms. They reach far behind the façades of enhanced security and dig deep trenches of questioning and mistrust even in families; they cause conflicts between parent and child; ecological conflicts are seen differently by men and women and may even complicate courtship, possibly condensing into the social stigmatization of certain people, professional groups, and companies, or into neuroses, both individual and collective. All this happens without any obvious damage to the façades of action, decision making, and assertion.

Therefore, a policy of lip service to ecology becomes completely indispensable; industrial self-damage may continue, but only unacknowledged, unaccountably, and with the full blessing of conservationists. But that also means that the central line of the conflict does run between those for and those against ecologically conscious production and politics; instead the general "for" is polarized into, on the one hand, a cosmetic and symbolic "for" that leaves causes untouched and sets the acknowledgment switches to "obstruct" and "shift," and, on the other, a "for" that intends to avoid the consequences even before they come into existence.

VIII

Riches are tangible goods that are present in everyday understanding even when they become abstract in the form of money. The perception of ecological devastation and the consequences of industrial growth, on the other hand, depend on methodological knowledge, measurement procedures, and rules of accountability and acknowledgment in science and law, and also on the usually defensive information policies of the suspect operations and the cooperating authorities. The perception of devastation must break through walls of denial. No matter how this happens, it is only rarely possible without crucial assistance from experts, that is, alternative experts, so we are dealing with conflicts that polarize professional rationality. The splitting of professional assessments is the prerequisite for and the agent of ecological conflicts and ecological consciousness.

At the same time, the type and scope of intraprofessional conflicts are indicators of the depth and stability of the foundation for an ecologically aware praxis. Are the "deviant" experts still publicizing their assessments one at a time, in isolation, or are they beginning to be organized, commanding their own means of presenting themselves? Can these experts conduct institutionalized research? Do they occupy positions on committees? Are they establishing careers? One is less concerned here with the direct integration of ecological viewpoints and more with working out and applying alternative solutions to the problem of accountability and acknowledgment. Physicians have to reveal dioxin-caused illnesses not just as individual patients' physical problems but as a social and political problem as well, and bring *that* into the public sphere. Scientists must resist denying the causes of consequences and must suggest and test rules of accountability that do justice to the International of devastation.

What is decisive is the "causal architecture" of the revealed threat at the time of its public and political discussion. Causality may in principle be unclear, ambiguous, and insoluble, but in fact one substance, one product, one industrial sector will end up holding the baby in the ecological repression race. Universal causality comes in the end to one, individual, cause; that is the modern sacrificial ritual of symbolic environmental policy. Take forest destruction as an example: what causes the problem is not the lack of a speed limit, not truck traffic, not coal-fired power plants, but passenger cars and ultimately—following the old industrial formula—the lack of a catalytic converter.

This is how, couched in scientific statements, the switches are set for social (in)action.

At the moment, this type of definitional struggle is raging to determine the central cause of ecological devastation, with population growth as the prime candidate. If population growth is determined to be the villain, then we in the wealthy, developed countries are finally off the hook for the devastation of the earth and can pass the buck to the Third World.

IX

Another essential difference from the old industrial conflict lies in the fact that, in the ecological conflict, individuals or tiny groups can act with quite considerable effect. It is curious if not paradoxical that, faced with the looming industrial catastrophe, nation-states become islands of helplessness, while opportunities arise for an almost individualistic "judo politics," which turns the consequences of industrial dominance—for instance, the fact that hazardous substances are almost omnipresent—against that dominance itself.

Consider a current conflict. In Germany, the soil in industrial areas is contaminated with far beyond the acceptable levels of dioxin, which increases the probability of cancer, particularly for children and infants who play on the ground. Publicizing the pollution and the threat, as well as setting acceptable pollution levels (levels that would take into account the general uncertainty) would set loose a political shock that might even help to bring about a bit of preventive policy—with effects on other topics and countries.

This unbinding of politics in risk society does not mean that collective action in politics would be superfluous. On the contrary, changing the accountability rules needs the sanctioning power of large-scale politics. But the opportunities for political action multiply themselves. Places and agencies that once seemed to act only under objective constraints become subpolitical centers, which in the prevailing dependence of everyone on everyone cannot be seamlessly controlled; nor can they act on their own authority. They are quite capable, however, of raising and fomenting preventive alternatives that publicize the institutions' failure to work toward prevention.

To put it in yet another way, the politics of the ecological question involve universal themes. The conflict even passes through people. While one's heart may beat Green, one's mind and routine often enough continue in old habits. All of this forms the background for an upheaval that can ultimately be completed only with everyone's cooperation.

Like the rich man through the eye of a needle, ecological revolutions must pass through each individual's rethinking and changing of even the smallest actions. Certainly, there are general objectives, general limiting conditions, and general risks of failure. But these can only be achieved or avoided in the millipede revolution of many million small steps, from above and below, in which the possibilities of an ecological expansion of democracy are tested and fought for.

X

This once again raises the question of the political subject. Is the individual, by opposing chemical technology, now supposed to be able to roll the stone back up the hill? No. As I said before, the ecological conflict scenario releases a political reflexivity in the risk conflict. Political reflexivity certainly doesn't favor ecological oppositional action, but it quite effectively irritates institutions. It can overturn the foundations of business plans or industrial authority, destabilize certainties, short-circuit separate spheres of action, and surreptitiously re-link old antagonisms. In short: involuntarily and against the prevailing order, the ossified system of industrial proclamations and excuses begins to move, and in this wind, this storm, the sailboats of ecological enlightenment may also cruise, sometimes with the wind and sometimes against it.

The environmental movement owes its success to the use, whether semi-naive or intentional, of this political reflexivity, in which are gathered the arguments of the ecological conflict: the objectivized power of accidents and whitewashed threats; the cardinal mistake of threat administration; the double game of those who both guarantee and threaten the highest public values; the peculiar constraints that result even from victories in the contest to distribute threats away; the fragility of any security that is suspended on the silver filaments of changeable knowledge.

XI

Why is nothing happening, or why isn't more happening? And this time a question as answer: What does it mean for everyday life to believe the problems exist and to take them seriously? Our own experience supports action on the social question: though poverty can be shot through with definitions or made to disappear statistically, it always remains painfully and physically present for those who must endure it. By contrast, the ecological issue is not merely abstract; it virtually requires that we ignore our own senses. Often the menace can only be perceived in defiance of the semblance of normality.

Only with the help of complicated, and usually expensive, measuring instruments and methods can the nature and degree of the threat be determined. Thus, in a sense, threats replace individual organs of perception with governmental, bureaucratic, and scientific "organs." Eyes become research institutes, ears become health authorities, and hands (washing themselves in innocence) become environmental ministries (and it is true here as well that one hand does not know what the other one is doing). By acknowledging the "toxin of the week," people unconsciously relinquish their own judgment in favor of the authorities'. Putting it another way, hiding from the threat is a kind of civilian defense. Self-confidence and the belief in the sovereignty of the senses, which are the fundamental virtue of democracy, rebel against the incapacitating, intimidating external definition of uncontrollable floods of threat. In the end, everyone only needs to do the most natural thing in the world—trust their own eyes—and the specter seems to disappear back whence it came, into nothingness.

Self-expropriation of the senses versus acceptance of imperceptible and obviously unpreventable threats—this is the central dilemma that the mobile pluralism of threats causes for everyday life. If this dilemma is not resolved, then initiatives directed against the institutions will accomplish nothing because they sanction, rather than oppose, the incapacitation of citizens.

What people see or do not see is not determined by their visual acuity, nor does it depend on their attentiveness, it is essentially codetermined by what they know or do not know. Knowledge unblocks the view. Someone who knows more and different things also sees more, sees differently, and sees different things. Where it is culturally possible to know which creatures suffer in which way from the general air pollution, that also becomes visibly recognizable. For example, the symptoms of dying trees are perceived, even if the authorities stifle discussion about the extinction of species, or call extinction by some other name.

The blindness of everyday life with respect to the omnipresent, abstract, scientific threats is therefore a relative and revisable process that depends on the socially available knowledge, on how one visualizes that knowledge based on one's own experience, and on whether and how much society considers it worthwhile to pay attention to these events that "at first glance" appear to be acting in a closed space. To emphasize an extreme view: in a society that devotes its highest attention to the industrial devastation of life, possibilities of knowledge are worked out and distributed and ways of acting are rewarded that simply raise into view what was previously invisible and thus make it assessable by everyone, at least in its outlines and fundamentals, because only in that way can democracy be protected from perishing in the thicket of risk expertocracy. Those who would open people's eyes to the ecological issue and keep them open must redirect and inspire society's knowledge and perception, that is, its education and training.[5]

There are good reasons to assume that the microcosm of daily behavior and dealings with oneself and others corresponds to the macrocosm of threat production. Such parallels are, for the most part, unconsidered and uninvestigated; but one can speculate, for instance, that a population that takes on the drudgery of sorting garbage daily would show little tolerance for the production of avalanches of garbage, and that the dirty issue of garbage would therefore become a lighting rod for democratic anger. Conversely, one can imagine that the acceptance of the everyday brutality of traffic paves the way for accepting the next nuclear accident. Traffic policy is cultural policy: practice in accepting everything, come what may.

It is not just the loss of something, but the lack of memory of the loss that buries it a second time and for good. Memory, however, which keeps what was lost from disappearing into oblivion, means cultural search and reliving. Anyone who, enclosed in the fleeting present, ignores the past just because it is past and does not keep the horizon of alternatives alive and open—whether in his or her own life, in a look at the landscape, or in politics—will lose the loss along with the memory, and perhaps even the pain of it, which is the mother of protest.

Nature is mute, certainly, and yet plants, for instance, can begin to talk for the attentive observer—quite without speech, entirely from the human activity and observation. The natural environment thus becomes a world of signs and symptoms, a mirror, an image for sensibilities and events that remain closed to the eye by itself (whatever that might be), but not to the knowing eye, which has learned, as Goethe put it, "to read in the book of nature."

XII

It is not the extinction of species that draws our attention to the extinction of species; protest against extinction is essentially also an echo of its showcasing in the major magazines and on the evening television screen. Only if nature is brought into people's everyday images, into the stories they tell, can its beauty and its suffering be seen and focused on.

Seeing is cultural seeing, attention is narrated attention. Our culture, and therefore we ourselves, see and hear in symbols, in which what is invisible or forgotten stands out and lives figuratively. This does not just happen; rather, it is done; it is work, art, mainly editorial work, often against resistance. Knowledge of cultural sensitivities is just as significant for this work as are courage and objective knowledge. Political reflexivity must be triggered and motivated by illustration, that is, by the editorial arrangement of the program, by the rebellious raising of questions in the media of the manufactured public sphere.

This all presumes that *experience* will once again be possible and legitimate in society—in science and particularly against it. For some time now, science has not been based on experience; it has become an experimental, methodological, and manufacturing science, whose triumph, according to its own understanding of itself, relies precisely on excluding and devaluing experience on the grounds that it is a subjective source of uncertain sensory data. Science has risen to its present dominating image of technical power and objectivity by virtue of its repression of experience, so to speak. Experience—understood as the individual's sensory understanding of the world—is the orphan child of the scientized world. Experience, which was once the main authority and judge of truth, has become the quintessence of the subjective, a relic, a source of illusions that attack the understanding and make a fool of it. In this view, it is not science but rather the subject and subjectivity that are wrong. According to its own ideal, science would be just as perfect as its technique, which must exclude the human being if it is concerned with managing the threats put into circulation by science.

But in social experience the protest against the destructive blindness of the industrial machinery makes itself heard. Personal science even learns continuously from public empirical science about the latter's own consequences and repressed sources of error (though not without a lot of help and obstinate resistance).

In fact, two divergent types of science are beginning to emerge in threat civilization: the science of data and the science of experience. The older, laboratory science, penetrates the world—by now down to the very center of the genetic code—by mathematical analysis but without experience; the other, this public discursivity based on experience, controversially uncovers objectives and means, consequences and threats.

Each has its own special perspectives, shortcomings, compulsions, and methods. The science of experimental data and laboratories can never wipe out the uncertainties accompanying probabilities that exclude nothing, and it is blind to the consequences that accompany and threaten its successes. A public forum on hazards, on the other hand, is in touch with everyday life and saturated with experience, but it is also dependent on the media and subject to manipulation and hysteria; and, in any case, it lacks a laboratory; that is, it depends on research and argumentation and requires a science that serves it (the traditional task of the universities!) in order to raise long-suppressed questions and to keep them focused, even against resistance. Thus it is a science of questions, not answers. It can also publicly test objectives and standards by sending them through a gauntlet of opposing opinion, and in that way it can stir up and enliven doubts that standard science with its blindness to threats and consequences, chronically ignores. A completely different type of knowledge is involved in the two sciences. In one, it is specialized, complex, and dependent on methodology. In the other, it is oriented toward essential features and fundamental mistakes (for instance, to the problem of setting acceptable levels of pollution or toxicity, where errors can never be corrected for the individuals affected—this is crucial knowledge). Its goal would be to break the dictatorship of laboratory science, very much in the Spirit of Popper, by giving the public a say in science and publicly raising questions, which would also have to be directed against the narrow-mindedness of everyday consciousness and the mass media.

This public experiential science (which is already active but which must be further organized), accepted as legitimate knowledge and authorized to make decisions, would have the function of an "open upper house of parliament." It would have to ask "How do we wish to live?" and it would have to hold the answers up as the standard for scientific plans and consequences. Only by developing such a science in a controversial and controlled manner, in opposition to the closed circles of laboratory science, could the voices of law, politics, and, not least, ordinary citizens and daily life develop their own judgment against the dominance of experts (or opposing experts). Just as was once done to the legal transcendence of monarchies, one could establish a division of powers and democratically monitor and oppose the technocracy of threat.

XIII

All this might be considered idealistic, abstract, impossible, technocratic, and, most probably, merely contrived. I am not able or willing to meet all these objections here. There is a lot of resistance to the transformation, whether in large or in small steps, from a scientifically inspired policy of revealing horror scenarios to a social-science-based redirection of accountability. However, it also seems to me to open the possibility of regaining the political initiative and thus finding an urgently needed response to the world contest between mega-risks for the title of most promising prospect of doom.

The ecological movement and the Greens are split over whether the size and urgency of the threats oblige us to take technocratic corrective action. At five minutes to midnight, some fear, it is no longer possible to consider rights to liberty or the long-obsolete ideals of the Enlightenment. I think there is a conceptual mistake here. The secret elective affinity between the ecologization and the democratization of society is not being recognized. The long-term policy toward threats should be: slowing down, revisability, accountability, and, therefore, the ability for consent as well; that is to say, the expansion of democracy into previously walled-off areas of science, technology, and industry. The *opportunities* of risk society are not being recognized or utilized.[6] What is important is to exploit and develop the superiority of doubt against industrial dogmatism. The goal is not a turning back but rather a *new modernity*, which would demand and achieve self-determination, and prevent its truncation in industrial society.

Notes

1. See the essay by Klaus Dörre, "Schafft sich autoritäre Technokratie selbst ab? Oder: Welche 'Gegengifte' braucht die 'Risikogesellschaft'?" in Ulrich Beck, *Politik im der Risikogesellschaft* (Frankfurt a.M.: Suhrkamp Verlag, 1991) (the German original of the present translation), pp. 232ff.
   translation), pp. 232ff.
2. See Claus Offe, "Selbstbeschränkung als Methode und als Resultat," in Beck, *Politik in der Risikogesellschaft*, pp. 225ff.
3. Sociology is *the* science (and perhaps the only one, together with the historical and political science of the "social question") that can break open, investigate, and argue against the inability to act caused by the constraints of disciplines that focus rigidly on nature; more cautiously, it could do this by regaining sociohistorical perspective and diagnostic power. It is charged with working out the theory of the changeability of those who oppose industrial society and its institutions, which block the necessary ecological reformation in thought and action. The "modernization of modern societies," the theme of the Sociologist's Convention in 1990, means fundamentally the modernization of industrial societies. Modernity and industrial society designate poles of an antagonism and a conflict of which we are only gradually becoming aware. Enlightenment (that is, the liberation from uncomprehended compulsions), democracy, and humanity are the measures against which unleashed industrialism fails. Having grown together with industrial society even to the level of the outline of its controversies, sociology is called to a revision of its premises and theories in the face of the ecological challenge—or it will stand and fall with the mistakes of

industrial society; on this see pp. 133ff.

4. Thomas Hobbes, *Leviathan* (Frankfurt, 1980), p. 194. Translated back from the German.

5. On this, see Bernhard Claußen, "Politische Bildung in der Risikogesellschaft: Ein politigischer und fachdidaktischer Problemaufriß," in Beck, *Politik in der Risikogesellschaft*, pp. 330ff.

6. See Thomas Schmid, "Die Chancen der Risikogesellschaft," in Beck, *Politik in der Risikogesellschaft*, pp. 216ff.

2

Survival Issues, Social Structure, and Ecological Enlightenment

ARE RISKS TIMELESS?

Aren't risks at least as old as industrialization, possibly as old as the human race? Isn't all life subject to the risk of death? Aren't all societies and all epochs "risk societies"? Shouldn't we acknowledge that threats—famines, epidemics, or natural catastrophes—have been continually reduced since the beginning of industrialization? Think of the reduction in infant mortality, the achievements of the welfare state, the enormous progress in technological perfection over the past hundred years. Isn't Germany, in particular, an El Dorado of bureaucratically organized care and caution?

There are certainly "new" risks, such as nuclear power, chemical and biotechnical production, and the like. But aren't these dangers, of potentially great scope, considered mathematically or physically, also of exceedingly small, in fact negligible, probability? And therefore, considering them coolly and rationally, shouldn't we worry about them even less than we worry about long-accepted risks, such as the incredible carnage on the highways or the risks to smokers?

Absolute security is denied to us human beings. But isn't it also true that the unavoidable "residual risks" are the downside of the historically unparalleled opportunities—for prosperity, relatively high social security, and general comfort—that advanced industrial society offers to most of its members? In the end, isn't the dramatization of such risks a typical media spectacle that ignores established expert opinion,

19

a "new German anxiety"? And finally, aren't risks primarily the concern of engineering and the physical sciences? What business has the sociologist here?

THE CALCULUS OF RISKS: PREDICTABLE SECURITY IN THE FACE OF AN OPEN FUTURE

Humanities' dramas—plagues, famines, and natural disasters, the looming power of gods and demons—may or may not quantitatively equal the destructive potential of modern mega-technologies. They differ essentially from "risks" in my sense since they are *not the result of decisions*, or more precisely, of decisions that focus on techno-economic advantages and opportunities and accept threats as simply the dark side of progress. This is my first point: risks presume industrial, that is, techno-economic, decisions and considerations of utility. They differ from war damage in that they originate in peacetime in the centers of rationality and prosperity, and from preindustrial natural disasters in that they originate in decision making. Decision making, of course, is never conducted solely by individuals but, rather, by entire organizations and (political) groups.[1]

Thus, there is a fundamental difference: preindustrial threats, no matter how large and devastating, were "strokes of fate" raining down on humanity from and attributable to some "other"—gods, demons, or nature. There were countless recriminations for the catastrophes, but they were directed against the gods or God; they were religiously motivated, to put it simply, but—unlike the recriminations that accompany industrial risks—they were not politically charged. With the beginning of decision making, the problem of social accountability and responsibility within society irrevocably arose, even where the prevailing rules in science and the law only allow accountability in exceptional cases. People, businesses, state agencies, and politicians are responsible for industrial risks. As we sociologists say, the social roots of risks block the "externalizability" of the problem of accountability.[2]

Therefore, it is not the number of dead and wounded but rather a social feature, that they are industrially caused, that makes the consequences and hazards of mega-technology a political issue. Nevertheless, the question remains: Must one not assess the past two hundred years as a period of continual growth in the calculability and in the precautions for dealing with industrially produced insecurity or destruction? In fact, one important approach to the last two hundred years, barely explored to date, is to trace the (political) institutional history of industrial society as the conflict-laden emergence of a system of rules for dealing with industrially produced risks and insecurities.[3]

The idea of a collective agreement as a response to the uncertainties that lie in opening and conquering new markets and in developing and implementing new technologies is hardly new. For example, insurance contracts, which charge the individual a general contribution while simultaneously freeing him from dramatic damage cases, originated as for back as the beginnings of intercontinental maritime trade, but with the growth of industrial capitalism, it was perfected and expanded into nearly all problematic areas of social action. Consequences that once affected only the individual became "risks," events that could be described systematically and statistically, and that were in this sense "calculable" and thereby amenable to supra-individual, political rules of recognition, settlement, and avoidance.

The calculus of risks connects the physical, the engineering, and the social sciences. It can be applied to completely disparate phenomena in the area of health management—from the risks of smoking to those of nuclear power—and also to economic risks, to the risks of old age, unemployment, traffic accidents, certain periods of life, and so forth. It permits a type of technological moralization which no longer directly employs moral and ethical imperatives. For example, mortality rates, under certain conditions of air pollution, replace the "Categorical Imperative." In this sense one can say that the calculus of risks exemplifies a type of morality without morality, the mathematical morality of the technological age. The triumph of the calculus of risks would probably not have been possible if there were not fundamental advantages to it.

The first advantage is that risks open the opportunity to statistically document consequences that were formerly "individualized," that is, borne by individuals. Statistical documentation reveals these consequences as events conditioned by the system and, accordingly, in need of general political regulation. Through the statistical description of risks (for example, in the form of tables showing accident probabilities), the mask of individualization drops off (something that has still not occurred sufficiently in the case of environmental diseases such as asthma or certain cancers). A field is opened for corresponding political action: accidents on the job, for instance, are not blamed on those whose health they have already ruined anyway but are tied to the plant's organization, precautions, and so on.

A second advantage is closely connected to the first: insurance payments are agreed on and guaranteed on a no-fault basis (setting aside the extreme cases of gross negligence or intentional damage), and so legal battles over causation become unnecessary and moral outrage is moderated. Instead, businesses have an incentive for prevention, in proportion to the magnitude of the insurance costs—or at least, that is the hope.

The decisive advantage, however, is that the calculus of risk enables the industrial system to deal with its own unforeseeable future. The calculus of risks and protection by insurance promise the impossible: events that have not yet occurred can be addressed now—through prevention, compensation, or provisions for after-care. As the French sociologist François Ewald shows in detailed theoretical and historical studies, what is new about the risk-insurance formula is that it makes the incalculable calculable, with the help of accident statistics, through generally applicable settlement formulas and the generalized exchange principle of "money for damages."[4] In this way, a normative system of rules for social accountability, compensation, and precautions, always controversial in its details, creates present security in the face of an open, uncertain future. Modernity, which introduces uncertainty into all the niches of existence, is confronted by its counterprinciple in a "social pact," woven out of public and private insurance contracts, against industrially produced uncertainties and destruction.

This pact for containing and "justly" distributing the consequences of the Industrial Revolution is politically and programmatically somewhere between socialism and liberalism, because it is based on the systematic creation of consequences and threats while at the same time it involves individuals in preventing them and compensating for them. The consensus that can be achieved with this pact is always unstable, conflict-laden, and in need of revision. For that very reason, however, it represents a central part of the consensus on progress, its "social logic," which in principle legitimized techno-economic development in the first phase of industrialism. Where this "security pact" is violated wholesale and systematically, the consensus on progress itself is consequently up for grabs.

RISK AND THREAT: ON THE OVERLAPPING OF NORMAL AND EXCEPTIONAL SITUATIONS

My central premise, and the one that leads us further, is that this pact is being violated today in a series of technological challenges—nuclear power, many types of chemical and biotechnical production and continuing ecological devastation. These are subverting the foundations of established risk logic.[5]

Put another way: since the middle of this century the social institutions of industrial society have been confronted with the historically unprecedented possibility, brought about by our own decisions, of the destruction of all life on this planet. This distinguishes our epoch not only from the early phase of the Industrial Revolution but also from all other cultures and social forms, no matter how diverse and contradictory. If a fire breaks out, the fire brigade comes; if a traffic accident occurs, the insurance pays. This interplay between before and after, between security in the here-and-now and security in the future because one took precautions even for the worst imaginable case, has been revoked in the age of nuclear, chemical, and genetic technology. In their brilliant perfection, nuclear power plants have suspended the principle of insurance not only in the economic but also in the medical, psychological, cultural, and religious sense. The "residual risk society" is an uninsured society, in which protection, paradoxically, decreases as the threat increases.

No real institutions—and probably none conceivable—could be prepared for the "maximum credible accident," and no social order could guarantee the integrity of cultural and political structures for this worst case.[6] There are many institutions, however, that are expert in the only possible response, which is to deny the threats. Instead of provisions for after-care, which guarantee security even in danger, we have the dogma of infallibility, which denies that there could be any incident. The queen of error, science, becomes keeper of the taboo: only "Communist" reactors, not Western ones, are empirical creations of human hands that are capable of throwing all the scientists' theories into a cocked hat. Even the simple question, "But, what if?" points up the lack of any planning for after-care. Accordingly, political stability in risk societies is the stability of not thinking about such problems.

Put more precisely: nuclear, chemical, genetic, and ecological megahazards abolish the four supporting pillars of the calculus of risks. First, these threaten global, often irreparable damage that can no longer be limited; the concept of monetary compensation therefore fails. Second, for the worst imaginable accident, there can be no provision for aftercare; the security concept of monitoring results fails. Third, the "accident" loses its delimitations in time and space, and therefore its meaning. It becomes an "event" with a beginning and no end; it becomes an open-ended carnival of galloping, creeping, overlapping waves of destruction. But that implies fourth, that standards of normality, measuring procedures, and, therefore, the basis for calculating the hazards collapse, causing incomparable entities to be compared; calculation thus turns into obfuscation.

The problem of the incalculability of consequences and destruction becomes particularly vivid in the lack of accountability. In our society, the recognition and attribution of hazards takes place, scientifically and legally, according to the principle of causality, the polluter-pays principle. But what seems self-evident to engineers and lawyers has extremely dubious, paradoxical consequences in the realm of mega-hazards. Consider the legal proceedings, during the 1980s, against the lead crystal factory in Altenstadt in the Upper Palatinate.[7] Penny-sized flecks of lead and arsenic were falling on Altenstadt, and fluorine vapors were turning leaves brown, etching windows, and causing bricks to crumble away. Residents were suffering from skin rashes, nausea and headaches. For once there was no question where the trouble origi-nated: white dust was pouring visibly from the smokestacks of the fac-tory; a clear case. A clear case? On the tenth day of the trial, the presiding judge offered to drop charges in return for a nominal fine of DM 10,000—an outcome typical of cases involving environmental crimes in the Federal Republic (1985: 13,000 investigations; 27 convic-tions with prison terms, 24 of those suspended; the rest dropped).

How is that possible? It is not just the lack of laws and not merely the legendary shortcomings in applying them which protect the crimi-nals. The reasons lie deeper and cannot be eliminated by the appeals to the police and the lawmakers that issue ever more loudly from the ranks of environmentalists. Convictions are blocked by the very thing that was supposed to achieve them: the strict application of the indi-vidually oriented polluter-pays principle.

In the case of the lead crystal factory, no one could or did deny that a crime had been committed, but a mitigating factor came into play: there were three other glass factories in the vicinity, all emitting the same pollutants. Notice: the more pollution is committed, the less is committed; or more precisely, the more liberal the acceptable level of pollution, and the greater the number of smokestacks and discharge pipes emitting pollutants and toxins, the lower the "residual probabil-ity" that a culprit can be made responsible for the general sniffling and coughing; that is to say, the less pollution is produced. But at the same time—one does not exclude the other—the general level of contamination and pollution is increasing. Welcome to the real-life travesty of the hazard technocracy![8]

Organized irresponsibility rests fundamentally on a mismatch between centuries. The hazards to which we are exposed date from a different century than the promises of security that attempt to subdue them. Herein lies the foundation both for the periodic outbreak of the con-tradictions of highly organized security bureaucracies and for the pos-sibility of normalizing these "hazard shocks" over and over again. On the threshold of the twenty-first century, the challenges of the age of atomic, genetic, and chemical technology are being handled with concepts and recipes that are derived from the early industrial society of the nineteenth and early twentieth centuries.[9]

Is there an operational criterion to distinguish between risks and threats? Yes: Business itself identifies the limit of tolerability with economic precision by refusing to offer private insurance. Where the logic of private insurance disengages, where the economic risks of insurance appear too large or too unpredictable to insurance concerns, the boundary that separates "predictable" risks from uncontrollable threats has obviously been breached.

Breaching this boundary has two consequences. First, the *social* pillars of the calculus of risks fail; security degenerates into mere technical safety. The secret of the calculus of risks, however, is that technical and social components work together: limitation, accountability, compensation, provisions for after-care. These are now disengaged, and social and political security can be created solely by claiming that technology is so far advanced that no accident could possibly occur.

Second, the social contradiction between highly developed safety bureaucracies and the legalization of mega-risks despite the clear lack of after-care is central to the political dynamic. A society attuned to safety and health at all levels is confronted with threats and devastation that defy all precautions.

Two opposing lines of historical development are converging: a level of security founded on the perfection of techno-bureaucratic norms and controls, and the spread and challenge of historically new hazards that slip through all the meshes of the law, technology, and politics. This contradiction, which is social and political rather than technical, remains masked by the "mismatch between centuries" (Günther Anders), and will continue to be hidden so long as the industrial patterns of rationality and control last. It will break down to the extent that the improbable event becomes probable. "Normal catastrophes" is the name Charles Perrow gives in his book to the predictability with which what had been ruled out occurs; and the more emphatically its possibility is denied, the sooner, more destructively, and more shockingly it occurs. Governmental and industrial authority's claim, based on technology, that everything is under control shatters when faced with a chain of publicly revealed catastrophes, near-catastrophes, whitewashed security failures and scandals—quite independently of the usual measures of threats: the number of dead, the danger of the contamination, and so on.[10]

The central social-historical and political potential of ecological, nuclear, chemical, and genetic hazards lies in the fact that these hazards threaten everyone with the collapse of administration, of techno-scientific and legal rationality, and of institutional, political guarantees of security; the potential lies in unmasking the real anarchy that has grown out of the denial that mega-threats are socially produced and administered.[11]

The threats of the nuclear and chemical age, therefore, have a social as well as a physical explosivity. As these threats appear, the institutions that are responsible for them, and then again not responsible, are forced to compete with their own security claims, a competition from which they can only emerge as losers. Some institutions are permanently under pressure to make even the safest things safer; but this overtaxes expectations and focuses attention so that in the end not only accidents but even the suspicion of them can cause the façades of safety claims to collapse. The other side of the recognition of threats is the failure of the institutions that derive their justification from the nonexistence of threat. Thus the "social birth" of a threat is an event that is equally improbable and dramatic, traumatic and unsettling, to the entire society.

Precisely because of their social and political explosiveness, threats remain distorted objects, ambiguous and interpretable, like modern mythological creatures that appear now to be an earthworm, now a dragon, depending on one's perspective and interests. The ambiguity of risks is also based in the revolutions that their official unambiguity provokes. The institutions of developed industrial society—politics, law, engineering sciences, industrial concerns—command a broad arsenal for "normalizing" noncalculable hazards. They can underestimate them, compare them out of existence, or excise their causal and legal identity. The instruments of a symbolic antipollution policy enjoy great significance and popularity.[12]

Ministers of the environment, no matter what their party affiliation, are not to be envied. Hampered by the scope of their ministry and its financial endowment, they must keep the causes largely constant and counter the inexorable destruction in a primarily symbolic fashion. A "good" minister of the environment is one who stages activities in a publicity-grabbing way, piling up laws, creating bureaucratic jurisdictions, centralizing information. He may even dive into the Rhine with a daredevil smile or try a spoonful of contaminated whey powder, provided the media eyes of a frightened public are trained upon him.

CONFLICT SCENARIOS; OR, THE SEARCH FOR ECOLOGICAL STRUCTURAL ANALYSIS

If risk society does not mean a purely technical challenge, then the question arises: What political dynamics, what social structures, what conflict scenarios arise from the legalization and normalization of systematic global and uncontrollable threats? To reduce things to an admittedly crude formula: hunger is hierarchical. Even in World War II, not everyone went hungry. Nuclear contamination, however, is egalitarian and in that sense "democratic." Nitrates in the groundwater do not stop at the general director's water faucet.[13]

Until now, all the suffering, all the misery, all the violence inflicted by people on other people recognized the category "the Other"—workers, Jews, blacks, asylum seekers, dissidents, and so on—and those apparently unaffected were safely outside this category. *The advent of nuclear and chemical contamination has let us experience the "end of the Other," the end of all our carefully cultivated opportunities for distancing ourselves.* Poverty can be marginalized, but not the threats of the age of nuclear, chemical, and genetic technology. This is where their peculiar and novel political force lies. Their power is the power of threat, which eliminates all the protective zones and social differentiations within and between nation-states.

It may be true that in the storm tide of threat we're all in the same boat, as the cliché goes. But as is so often the case, here, too, there are captains, passengers, helmsmen, machinists, and men and women overboard. In other words, there are countries, sectors, and enterprises that *profit* from the production of risk and others that find their economic existence and their physical well-being threatened. If, for instance, the Adriatic or the North Sea dies or is perceived by society as "hazardous to health"—this distinction is moot with respect to economic effects—then it is not just the North Sea or the Adriatic which dies, along with the life it contains and makes possible. The economic life of all the towns, sectors, and coastal countries that live directly or indirectly from the commercialization of the sea is also extinguished. At the tip of the future, which we can begin to see over the horizon of the present, industrial civilization is transformed into an international struggle for supremacy in the global risk society. The destruction of nature and the destruction of markets coincide here. It is not what one has or is able to do that determines one's social position and future, but rather where and how one lives and to what extent others are permitted, in a prearranged unaccountability, to pollute one's possessions and abilities in the guise of "environment."

Even passionate denial, which can certainly count on full official support, has its limits. The revenge of the abstract dispute among experts about threats is the geographic concretion of threats. Disputing everything, operating the official whitewashing machinery in high gear, does not prevent the devastation; it only accelerates it. Toxin-absorbing regions emerge, crossing national boundaries and old institutional lines of conflict and creating geographical areas whose fate coincides with the industrial destruction of nature.[14]

The Greenhouse Effect, for example, will raise temperatures and sea levels around the world through the melting of the polar icecaps. The warming will submerge entire coastal regions, turn farmland into desert, shift climatic zones in unpredictable ways, and dramatically accelerate the extinction of species. The poorest in the world will be hit the hardest. They will be least able to adapt themselves to the changes in the environment. Those deprived of the basis of their economic existence will flee the site of their misery; an exodus of eco-refugees and climatic asylum seekers will flood across the wealthy North; crises in the Third and Fourth Worlds could escalate into war. Even the climate of world politics will change at a faster pace than is imaginable today. So far, these are all just possibilities, but we must take them seriously. When they have become reality, it will already be too late to take action.

Many of these problems would be ameliorated if the countries on the way to industrialization could be spared the mistakes made by the highly industrialized countries. But unchecked expansion of industrial society is still considered the *via regia* that promises mastery of many problems—not just the problems of poverty—so that concern for the prevailing misery often displaces concern for abstract issues of environmental destruction.

"Threats to nature" are not just that; pointing them out also threatens property, capital, jobs, trade union power, the economic foundation of whole sectors and regions, and the structure of nation-states and global markets. Put another way: there is a major distinction, to which we are just beginning to become sensitive in sociology, between the conflict field of wealth production, from which the nineteenth century derived the experience and premises of industrial and class society, and the conflict field of hazard production in the nuclear and chemical age. The distinction probably lies in the fact that wealth production produced the antagonisms between capital and labor, while the systematic chemical, nuclear, and genetic threats bring about polarizations within capital—and thus also within labor—that cut across the social order. Just as the social welfare state had to be forced through against the concerted resistance of private investors, who were called to pay in the form of wage and fringe-benefit costs, so ecological threats split the business camp. At first glance, it is impossible to discern where and how the boundary runs, or, more accurately, who gets the power, and from where, to cause the boundary to run in what way.

While it may still be possible to speak of the environment on the level of an individual company, this talk becomes simply fictitious on the level of the overall economy, where a type of Russian roulette is being played under the increasingly thin cover of the environment. If it is suddenly revealed and publicized in the mass media (information policy becomes ever more important since threats are generally imperceptible in everyday life) that certain products contain certain "toxins" (according to the prevailing definitional norms—which depend on law and scientific rules of causality), then entire markets may collapse, and invested capital and labor power are instantly devalued.

No matter how abstract the threats may be, in the long run their concretizations are irreversible and regionally identifiable. What is denied collects itself into geographical areas, into "loser regions" which have to pay with their economic existence for the damage and its unaccountability. In this "ecological expropriation," we are facing the historical novelty of a devaluation of capital and work, while the ownership and sometimes even the characteristics of the goods remain constant. Sectors that have nothing or very little to do causally with the production of the threat—agriculture, the food industry, tourism, fisheries, the retail trade, and parts of the service industry—are also among those most affected.

Where the (world) economy splits into risk winners and risk losers, this polarization will also make its mark upon the structure of employment. First, new types of antagonisms that are specific to countries, sectors, and enterprises will arise between groups of employees and within and between trade-union organizations. Second, these antagonisms are, so to speak, third-hand antagonisms, derived from those between factions of capital, which turn the "fate of workers" into "fate" in a further and fundamental dimension. Third, with the intensified consciousness of these lines of conflict, sector-specific alliances may arise between the old class enemies, labor and capital. The consequences may be a confrontation between this union-management bloc and other mixed factions over and above the trenches of class differences that have narrowed under the pressure of "ecological politicization."[15]

One must imagine what this could mean for workers and unions. The production and definition of threats is aimed largely at the level of products, which is almost completely outside the influence of the works councils and workers' groups and falls completely under the jurisdiction of management. And this is still the intra-organizational level. Hazards are produced by business operations, to be sure, but they are defined and evaluated socially—in the mass media, in the experts' debates, in the jungle of interpretations and jurisdictions, in courts, or with strategic-intellectual dodges—in a context, that is to say, to which the majority of workers are totally alien. We are dealing with scientific battles waged over the heads of the workers and fought out, instead, by intellectual strategies in intellectual milieus. The definition of threats largely eludes the control of workers and even of trade unions. Workers and unions are not even the ones most affected (businesses and management are those primarily affected), but as secondary targets they must count on losing their jobs if worst comes to worst. Even a latent risk definition hits them squarely in their pride in achievement, their promise of a usable commodity. Labor and labor power can no longer regard themselves solely as the source of wealth; they must also get used to being perceived socially as a force for threat and devastation. The labor society is not only running out of jobs, which are what give meaning and solidity to life in that society, as Hannah Arendt ironically put it; it is also threatening even this residual meaning.[16]

Somewhat crudely, one can say in conclusion: What is "environment" for the polluting industry is the basis of economic existence for the afflicted regions and loser sectors. As a consequence, political systems in their architecture as nation-states, on the one hand, and large-scale ecological conflict positions, on the other, become mutually autonomous and create geopolitical shifts that place the structure of domestic and international economic and military blocs under completely new stresses but that also offer new opportunities. The phase of risk-society politics that is beginning to make itself heard today in the arena of disarmament and detente in the East-West relationship can no longer be understood nationally, but only internationally, because the social mechanics of risk situations disregard the nation-state and its alliance systems. In that sense, apparently ironclad political, military, and economic constellations are becoming mobile, and this forces, or permits, a new transnational "European domestic policy" (Genscher).

POLITICAL REFLEXIVITY: THE COUNTERFORCE OF THREAT AND THE OPPORTUNITIES FOR INFLUENCE BY SOCIAL MOVEMENTS

Where progress and doom seem to be interwoven, the goals of social development are antithetical on all levels. This is certainly not the first conflict that modern societies have had to master, but it is one of the most fundamental. Class conflicts or revolutions change power relations and exchange elites, but they hold fast to the goals of techno-economic progress and clash over civil rights that both sides recognize. The double face of self-annihilating progress, however, produces conflicts that cast doubt on the social bases of rationality—science, law, and democracy. Society is thus placed under permanent pressure to negotiate foundations without a foundation of its own. It experiences an institutional destabilization, in which all decisions—from local government policy on speed limits, to the details of industrial manufacturing, to the basic issues of energy supply, law, and technological development—can suddenly be drawn into fundamental political conflicts.

While the surface remains the same, quasi-governmental power positions arise in the research laboratories, nuclear power plants, chemical factories, editorial offices, courts, and so on, in the context of threats that depend on definitions and publicity. As the contradictions of the security state are stirred up, systems come to require action and become subject-dependent. The courageous Davids of this world get their chance. The fact that definitions of threat are so interdependent—impacting on markets, property rights, trade-union power, and political responsibility—implies that the institutions and individuals charged with making and publicizing them also cross boundaries in the social and political hierarchy.

One can use all one's powers of persuasion to pile up the institutional arguments for the nonexistence of suicidal threats; one need not deny a single iota of hope to the institutional hegemony; one can even draw on the distraction of the social movements and point out the limitations of their political effectiveness. Yet one must still recognize that this is all countered by the opposing power of threat. It is constant and permanent, it is not tied to interpretations that deny it, and it even exists in arenas where demonstrators have long since become exhausted. The probability of improbable accidents grows with time and the number of mega-technologies implemented. Every "event" arouses memories of all the other ones, not only in Germany but all over the world.

Different types of revolutions—coup d'état, class struggle, civilian resistance, and so on—have been contrasted with each other, but they all have in common the empowering and disempowering of social subjects. Revolution as an autonomous process, a hidden, latent, permanent condition in which circumstances are involved against their own interests while political structures or property and power relations remain unchanged: this is a possibility that, to my knowledge, has neither been considered nor thought through. But it is precisely this conceptual schema into which the *social power of threat* fits. Threat is the product of the deed; it requires no political authorization, no authentication; it dresses itself in the robes of progress: science, increased productivity, easing of labor, employment. Once threat exists, awareness of it endangers all the institutions, from business to science, from law to politics, that have produced and legitimized it.

Where will the opposing forces come from? It is probably fruitless to expect the various subcultures and ecological movements to produce Marxian "revolutionary subjects." It feels good, of course, to appeal to reason with all the rigor at one's command, and it can do no harm, precisely because a realistic view of past experience has shown that it has very little effect. One could also create yet another group for the solution of global problems. Certainly, it is to be hoped that political parties will catch on.

If none of this is sufficient to stimulate alternative political action, however, there remains the threat's power to trigger political reflexivity.[17] Three Mile Island, Chernobyl, Hanau, Biblis, Wackersdorf: the global experiment in nuclear energy has become its own critic, illustrating its own flaws even more convincingly and effectively than opposing political movements could ever have managed on their own. This becomes clear not only in the worldwide, free, negative advertising at prime time and on the front pages of papers, but also in the fact that everyone between the Alpine cottages and the North Sea mudflats now understands and speaks the language of the nuclear critics. Of necessity, people have passed a kind of crash course in the contradictions of threat administration in the risk society: on the arbitrariness of acceptable levels and calculation procedures, on the unimaginability of long-term consequences, and on the ability of statistics to make them anonymous. They have acquired more information, more vividly and more clearly, than even the most hostile critique could have taught them.

The most enduring, convincing, and effective critics of nuclear energy are neither the demonstrators outside the fences nor the critical public, no matter how indispensable they may be. The most influential opponent of the threat industry is the threat industry itself.

The power of the new social movements has its base not just in themselves but also in the quality and scope of the contradictions that involve the threat-producing and administering industries in risk society. Those contradictions become public scandal through the needling of social movements. Thus, there is not only an autonomous process of threat suppression, but also opposing tendencies to reveal the suppression, even though they are much less marked and always depend on the civil courage of individuals and the vigilance of social movements. Catastrophes that touch the vital nerves of a society with a highly developed bureaucracy of safety and welfare arouse the sensationalist greed of the mass media, threaten markets, make sales prospects unpredictable, devalue capital, cause global shifts in markets, and set streams of voters in motion. The evening news exceeds even the fantasies of countercultural dissent; daily newspaper reading becomes an exercise in technology critique. The oppositional power of this unintentional revelation of threats depends, of course, on overall social conditions that only a few countries possess: parliamentary democracy, (relative) independence of the press, and advanced production of wealth in which for the majority of the population the invisible threat of cancer is more real than the possibility of undernourishment and famine.

In the cooperation from within and without, over and above the boundary lines between the sub-systems, there are also symptoms of strength, so far almost unnoticed. The most astonishing and perhaps least understood social phenomenon of the 1980s in Germany is the unexpected renaissance of a "tremendous subjectivity"—inside and outside the institutions.[18] It is no exaggeration to say that citizens' groups have taken the thematic initiative. It was they who put an endangered world on the social agenda, against the resistance of the established parties. Nowhere does this become as clear as in the specter of the "new unity" that is haunting Europe. The pressure to pay lip service to ecology is universal. It unites the Christian Social Union with the Communists, and the chemical industry with its Green critics. All products, absolutely all products, are "safe for the environment," to say the least. There are rumors that the chemical concerns plan to follow up on their full-page ads and reestablish themselves as a registered conservation association.

Admittedly, this is all just packaging and programmatic opportunism, with perhaps a little rethinking of goals now and then. It hardly changes the facts. Yet it is still true that the themes of the future, which are now on everyone's lips, did not originate in the farsightedness of leaders or in struggles in parliament—and certainly not in the cathedrals of power in business, science, and the state. These themes have been put on the social agenda, against the concentrated resistance of institutionalized ignorance, by entangled, moralizing groups and splinter groups fighting each other and plagued by doubts. Democratic subversion has won a quite improbable thematic victory in Germany, breaking with an authoritarian culture that has historically been prepared to obey any official nonsense or insanity.

Europe is called to a new social project and has already embarked on it. The ideological fortresses of the East-West antagonism are breaking up, and the international themes of risk civilization could move into the resulting vacuum. One sign of this is the pressure for global arrangements that technology, science, and business produce; another is the appearance of suicidal threats everywhere in the world; and yet another sign comes from the elevated standards of safety and rationality promised in developed welfare-state capitalism.

These are the opportunities that offer themselves to a type of European politics that would transcend the inherited distinctions between foreign and domestic policy and not only in founding and building a "European house": the highly industrialized countries must also assume a large share of the costs for the necessary corrective measures. Europe, where the dynamic of industrial development had its origin, could also be the birthplace of an enlightenment about and against industrial society. The struggle for an ecological enlightenment would have to be waged in both broad concepts and in small details; it would have to extend even to everyday life, because the threats overturn well-worn routines everywhere and represent a spectacular challenge for civil courage—on the job in industry; in physicians' practices where people come with their fears and questions; in research, which can obfuscate or reveal; in the courts; in the monitoring administration; and, not least, in the editorial offices of the mass media, which can make the invisible culturally discernible. There are many practical concerns in the relationship of the "European house" to its neighbors on this planet. What is important is that we stop acting with the arrogance of the charitable wealthy, and, instead, admit our destructive industrial role and correct it.

Notes

1. Niklas Luhmann has pointed out this difference between preindustrial hazards, which are not controllable but which also are not caused by decisions, and industrial risks, which come from decisions and utility considerations. Here Luhmann, the systems theorist, ascribes the decisions exclusively to individuals, who otherwise never occur inside organizations and bureaucracies in his theory. N. Luhmann, "Die Moral des Risikos und das Risiko der Moral," in G. Bechmann (ed.), *Risiko und Gesellschaft* (Opladen, 1993).

2. This occurs in a historical amalgam of nature and society, where even natural catastrophes such as floods, landslides, and the like, which are apparently externally caused, appear to be caused by human beings. On this point, see U. Beck, *Gegengifte. Die organisierte Unverantwortlichkeit* (Frankfurt a.M., 1988), chap. 2.

3. Important considerations on this point are found in F. Ewald, *L'Etat Providence* (Paris, 1986); and also in A. Evers and H. Nowotny, *Über den Umgang mit Unsicherheit* (Frankfurt a.M., 1987); G. Böhret (ed.), *Herausforderungen an die Innovationskraft der Verwaltung* (Opladen, 1987); K. M. Meyer-Abich, "Von der Wohlstands-zur Risikogesellschaft," *Aus Politik und Zeitgeschichte*

36 (1989): 3ff.; C. Lau, "Risikodiskurse," *Soziale Welt* 3 (1988): 418–436. A survey of the recent risk discussions crossing disciplinary boundaries is offered by M. Schütz (ed.), *Risiko und Wagnis*, 2 vols. (Pfüllingen, 1989).
4. Cf. Ewald, *L'Etat Providence.*
5. This idea was first worked out in case studies of major accidents by P. Lagadec, *Das grosse Risiko* (Nördlingen, French original, 1982), and deepened by Ewald, *L'Etat Providence*, and C. Perrow, *Normale Katastrophen* (Frankfurt a.M., 1988; English original, 1982). The argument was also developed in the German linguistic area by Evers and Nowotny, *Über den Umgang.* For details, see Beck, *Gegengifte*, as well as Lau, "Risikodiskurse."
6. The disputes over so-called catastrophic medicine this illustrates.
7. Reported in *Der Spiegel* 46 (1986): 32ff.
8. The debate over the duties and function of law in risk societies has increased in recent years: R. Wolf, "Die Antiquiertheit des Rechts in der Risikogesellschaft," *Leviathan* 15 (1987): 357–391; idem, " 'Herrschaft kraft Wissen' in der Risikogesellschaft," *Soziale Welt* 2 (1988): 164–187; K. M. Meyer-Abich and B. Schefold, *Die Grenzen der Atomwirtschaft* (Munich, 1986); E. H. Ritter, "Umweltpolitik und Rechtsentwicklung," *Neue Zeitschrift für Verwaltungsrecht* 11 (1987): 929–938; T. Blanke, "Autonomie und Demokratie," *Kritische Justiz* 4 (1986): 406–422; G. Heinz and U. Meinberg, "Empfehlen sich Änderungen im strafrechtlichen Umweltschutz, insbes. in Verbindung mit dem Verwaltungsrecht? Gutachten D für den 57. Dt. Juristentag," in Ständige Deputation des Dt. Juristentages (ed.), *Verhandlungen des 57. Dt. Juristentages in Mainz* (Mainz, 1988), vol. 1, part D; R. P. Calliess, "Strafzweck und Strafrecht. 40 Jahre Grundgesetz—Entwicklungstendenzen vom freiheitlichen zum sozial-autoritären Rechtsstaat?," *Neue Juristische Wochenschrift* 21 (1981): 1338–1343; and G. Bruggemeier, "Unwelthaftsrecht. Ein Beitrag zum Recht in der 'Risikogesellschaft,' " *Kritische Justiz* 2 (1988): 209–230.
9. In the sequel we will not be concerned only, nor primarily, with issues of a new ethics of civilizational action, but with the fact that the established categories and criteria for institutional action stem from a different world.
10. Günther Anders, *Die Antiquiertheit des Menschen: Über die Zerstörung des Lebens im Zeitalter der dritten industriellen Revolution* (2 vols, Munich, 1980); Charles Perrow, *Normal Accidents: Living with High Risk Technologies* (New York: Basic Book, 1984).
11. Until the accident at Chernobyl, protection against catastrophes, for example, was planned only within a radius of 29 km around a power plant; foreign accidents were officially excluded. See R. Czada and A. Drexler, "Konturen einer politischen Risikoverwaltung," *Österreichische Zeitschrift für Politikwissenschaft* 1 (1988): 52ff., as well as H. Gottweis, "Politik in der Risikogesellschaft," *Österreichische Zeitschrift für Politikwissenschaft* 1 (1988): 3ff.
12. This is shown vividly and from an inside perspective by J. Fischer, *Der Umbau der Industrielgesellschaft* (Berlin, 1989), pp. 29–54.
13. For extensive discussion of this, see U. Beck, *Risikogesellschaft. Auf dem Weg in eine andere Moderne* (Frankfurt a.M., 1986; English: *Risk Society* [London, 1992]), pp. 48ff. The conflicts and crises of classical industrial society have not ended, so overlaps will occur between the social structure and conflict dynamics of industrial and risk society. I exclude them here.
14. Cf. Beck, *Gegengifte*, pp. 247ff.

15. "That there are symptoms of such a bloc formation is seen in the West German nuclear industry following Chernobyl: works councils and employers' representatives jointly defended prevailing West German energy policy against any change of course." M. Schumann, "Industrielle Produzenten in der ökologischen Herausforderung," Research Proposal (Göttingen, 1987). Contrary to the prevailing assumptions, H. Heine and R. Mautz, in a study on "industrial workers against environmentalism," conclude: "With the trend to professionalization of production work in the chemical industry, chemical workers could in the future constitute a growing potential of ecologically vigilant production workers, who are capable of reflecting critically upon the ecological conditions and consequences of their own labor, and represent a supporting force for ecologically motivated political interventions," *Industriearbeter contra Umweltschutz* (Frankfurt a.M., 1989), p. 187.

16. H. Arendt, Vita Activa *Oder vom tätigen Leben* (Munich: R. Piper Verlag, 1960), 88.

17. This view is based generally on the theoretical distinction between simple and reflexive modernization, which has not yet been adequately worked out. To put it crudely, simple modernization runs within the framework of industrial-society categories and principles. Reflexive modernization is a phase of social transformation in which, by dint of its own dynamics, modernization changes shape. Class, stratum, occupation, sex roles, businesses, sectoral structures, and the general presuppositions and course of "natural" techno-economic progress are all affected. Classical industrial society is becoming just as much a tradition to be run over and demystified as, in the nineteenth century, industrial modernization ran over and demystified status-based feudal society. Unconsciously, and counter to planned activity, modernization is undercutting modernization. In that way, however, restratifications in social structures arise, along with power shifts, new lines of conflict, and possibilities and constraints for coalitions. Social movements, the public sphere, ethics, the civil courage of individuals, and political networks get their chance to exert historical influence. See "The Conflict of Two Modernities," chapter 11 in this volume.

18. See the discussion of individualization and social structure in Beck, *Risikogesellschaft*, chaps. 3 and 4, as well as U. Beck and E. Beck-Gernsheim, *Das ganz normale Chaos der Liebe* (Frankfurt a.M., 1990), pp. 11ff., 38ff., 108ff., and 189ff.

3

On the Mortality
of Industrial Society

People have begun to question modernity. It is not that they no longer appreciate its advantages or that they no longer know how to live in and from it. But its premises have begun to wobble. Many people are deeply upset over the house-of-cards character of superindustrialism. On the one hand, the sciences snipe at each other, using their characteristic precision to find more and more hairs in the soup they have fixed for themselves and for us, and a solid, scientifically founded epistemological skepticism is flourishing. On the other hand, the sciences fumble around, blurring the border between life and death, and, consciously or unconsciously, doing sums—in the ordinary routine of their institutes—with destructive forces that could turn the earth into a fireball many times over. Mistake? Human failure? Impossible!

Certainly one can find arguments in favor of superindustrialism, but there are arguments against it, too! It is really alarming that these arguments, no matter how uncertain they may be, only play a very minor role in the controversy. People quickly and aggressively swing the club of "international competitiveness" and the whip of "job security." Thus, we are not even able to reflect and decide whether we actually want and can endure the benefits that continue to revolutionize our lives, because, at the same time, we have to do something else: we have to ensure our position in world markets, our jobs, and the basis of our existence. The innovations that we start and that then roll over us like an alien power all take place while we pursue something else. We stand the world on its head, we tip nature over, we drain the lifeblood from traditions, and all the while we are concerned with something else, something simple and comprehensible. We must earn

37

our living, standing up to whatever competition in whatever market, according to its rules of behavior. The consequences are all too tangible: Germany is being wired for cable and is falling more and more under the sway of the media; innovations are continually introduced and implemented; all with a sweeping reference to the world market and the principle of maximizing jobs. Industrial progress, which has changed the face of the earth and which will continue to change it as no previous revolution ever has, is occurring as an unseen side effect of "business as usual"—without a plan, without political will or consciousness, and without any possibility of democratic participation. This revolution is the latent consequence of normalcy.

INDUSTRIAL ANARCHY?

It is the degree of this autonomization, coinciding with the new, far-reaching surges of modernization with their completely unpredictable consequences, that inspires the general discontent with modernity. Everyone is aware of techno-scientific innovations, particularly the micro-electronics revolution and the new means of communication, whose universal applicability will disrupt all the familiar structures of working, living, and communicating and create new ones, or at least make them possible. How we will cope with the immense advances in the biosciences is being discussed more and more frequently and vehemently in public. In other words, one revolution with the next; the microelectronics revolution links with the biological revolution, which links with the medical one, and so on. Soon we will be in the middle of a festival of slightly anarchic industrial revolutions. To judge by the results of the previous revolutions this will not provoke jubilation or tears of joy.

Undoubtedly, there are many basic improvements, in all areas of our life, that we cannot imagine doing without. In this sense, modernity has become second nature to us. But humanity has never before had to live so much under the threat of self-annihilation. Never before have entire oceans been threatened with poisoning. Never before have entire animal species disappeared from the face of the earth, almost overnight, through greed or carelessness. Never before has an artificial overheating of the atmosphere threatened world climate. There is no need to glorify the past to keep one's eyes open very wide to all the so-called side effects of modernization.

The public critique of modernity has largely been snagged on the issues in the area between science and technology. The "big secret" in the prevailing self-concept is technology. In technology are gathered all the forces that keep the motor of innovation running, transforming the still-new society into an old one. Religions may decline, cultures may collapse, nature may be dying—industrial-society man is virtually hypnotized by the machine. In it his creativity becomes tangible.

This fascination is especially obvious where industrial-society man risks losing control of technology, where utility and destruction go hand in hand. It is a paradox of modernity that it created a *social* system that assigns a central position to technology, and that thereby conceals its own sociality behind the façade and the fascination of technological processes. In particular, the debates of the past few decades, which have deployed the entire arsenal of arguments critical of technology and industry, have remained at heart technocratic and naturalistic. They exhaust themselves in exchanging and citing figures for pollutant levels in the air, water, and food, figures comparing population growth, energy consumption, nutritional requirements, raw material shortage, and so on, with as much ardor and intensity as if there had never been anyone—a certain Max Weber for instance—who (apparently) wasted his time proving that this debate is either senseless or vacuous, and probably both, unless one also considers society's power structures and distribution structures, its bureaucracies and its prevailing norms and thought patterns. A preconception has crept in and established itself by which modernity is truncated to the reference frame of technology and nature as perpetrator and victim. In the process, however, the very thing one had hoped to combat is involuntarily promoted. The possibilities for structuring technology remain hidden from this conception of modernity (as well as from the political environmental movement) behind the ideology of objective constraints, which is further strengthened by the technological opposition to technology. And is modernity really off the hook, so to speak, if wastewater is taken care of? Isn't humanity *implicitly* abolished once again if our concern is limited to modernity's impact on nature and health? isn't humankind then reduced to its biological basis—a reduction with which we in Germany are only too familiar?

CULTURAL AND SOCIAL MODERNIZATION

Considering this focus on technology and nature, it is hardly surprising that public consciousness is scarcely aware that modernization is a social and cultural process encompassing all areas of the individual's life in society. People protect themselves with a conception of nature versus society and its impenetrable jungle of issues. People's upset and insecurity are great, and, therefore, so is their tendency to make visible, tangible things the objects of argument and action: technology and nature, or gender, age, skin color, nationality. However, this tendency (which grows as our insecurity grows) to attribute problems to tangible things that can be personally experienced is deceptive.

No one who has been caught up in the stream of issues can confidently draw models for the future from the past. Are the models of family, marriage, femininity, masculinity, parenthood, education, occupation, and career—models that reliably guided life a generation or two ago—still productive for modeling one's own life and the life of the coming generation? Ultimately, what emerges from the fading social norms is naked, frightened, aggressive ego in search of love and help. In the search for itself and an affectionate sociality, it easily gets lost in the jungle of the self and thus becomes the plaything of social fashions and relationships. In this "individualization process," people fall out of the nest of binding and guiding traditions, "set free," in Marx's term, from the limits and securities of class cultures and traditional milieus; they are thus confronted with themselves as the pivots and hinges of their own lives. This very logic makes it difficult or impossible to recognize the social character of the individualization process. Someone who is poking around in the fog of his or her own self is no longer capable of noticing that this isolation, this "solitary-confinement of the ego" is a mass sentence, that millions of people, in all the highly industrialized countries, are also pacing the prison cells of the self.

INDIVIDUALIZATION AND CLASS FORMATION

We have reached a plateau in a sociohistorical process that began a good two hundred years ago, as the fragments and incrustations of status society and feudal agrarian cultures were overtaken, melted, and re-formed by the dynamicizing centers of the market, the division of labor, the finance economy, science, and technology. The term "modernization" has become established for this complex process in which one social form, industrial society, pushed another, feudal agrarian society, off the stage of world history. Modernization includes the surge of technological rationalization and the change in labor and organization, but it comprises much more than that: the transformation of social character and expected life paths, of lifestyles and forms of love, of power and influence structures, of political forms of repression and participation, of concepts of reality and epistemological norms. The plow, the steam locomotive, and the microchip are only external, visible indicators of a much deeper process that includes and transforms the entire social structure, a process that ultimately replaces our most firmly held convictions, the certainties from which life feeds, with new ones. Today, unlike in the nineteenth century, people are not crowded together and fused into large groups, socially and politically active "classes," by the pressure of poverty and tangibly experienced workplace alienation in rapidly growing cities bursting at the seams. On the contrary: against a background of the social and political protections and rights that have been fought for and won, people are removed from class connections and socio-moral milieus and more and more must rely on themselves to make a living and defend their rights. Cushioned by the welfare state, the modernization process, which once favored and brought about the formation of classes, has become an individualization of class cultures (with inequalities unchanged). In the social and political blast furnace that arose from the immiseration of the working masses in the uncontrollably growing cities, the political ideas and forms of struggle were forged that much later—in the boom phase after World War II—created conditions favoring individualistic ways of acting and thinking. Material poverty is confined to marginal groups; prosperity, quite modest in objective terms but considerable when compared to the conditions one's ancestors lived in, creates the long-awaited possibilities of privacy, family, and leisure. There has been a "democratization" of once-exclusive lifestyle opportunities. Domestic and neighborly closeness is replaced by an increased pluralization of lifestyles. Interests, now juridically protected, can be claimed individually. Mobility and educational opportunities proliferate and force people (removed from their traditional milieu and its protections) to stand on their own and conceive of themselves as the agents of their own labor market and personal fate; their objective dependence on sociality only appears occasionally and in refracted form.

"EVERYTHING WILL STAY THE SAME," AND SO WE SLIDE INTO A NEW SOCIETY

Compared to the waves of modernization that are in store for us, development so far has been harmless. My basic thesis is this: we are sliding into a *new* society, not a changed society, not a "postindustrial" or "late capitalist" society, but, rather, a novel social structure for which we have as yet no concept and thus no eye.

How is this to be understood? Modernity is said to be constantly innovating. *Modernity in this sense is a subpolitical "revolutionary system" without a revolutionary program or goal.* Modernity is a revolutionary-system wolf hidden in sheep's clothing of science, business, and technology. The classics of modernity have always known and said this, and yet made us forget it. In the fat, stable postwar years, this dynamic appeared to shut down in conformity to the system and was downplayed as "social transformation without transformation."

Like the feudally ossified agrarian society of the nineteenth century, however, industrial society today is beginning to move, after a restorative phase, and this movement originates from at least two centers. One is the development and implementation of new technologies, which not only completely remodel the production sectors but also reach into all areas of society (computers, microchips, telecommunications, news media). The other is the erosion of social and cultural traditions and ways of life (class, strata, occupation, family, marriage, gender roles). The new phase of social modernization, whose first waves are beginning to break over us today, is no longer just an "industrial" revolution, that is, a technological and economic revolution related to the production sector; it is also a social and cultural revolution that fragments and pluralizes the familiar social categories and forms of industrial society and fundamentally changes their significance for people's lives.

The political explosiveness of the coming decades lies precisely in the technological and social double character of this quasi-revolutionary modernization. The rug is being pulled out from under the reality and the political and social institutions of industrial society—trade unions, parties, state institutions, and educational, occupational, welfare, and family policy; again and again, new social movements venture into the detraditionalized voids that are being created. But this is precisely how the way is cleared for the implementation of new technologies that reach deeply into the structure of society. Three examples follow.

THE GOLIATH OF MICROELECTRONICS

The new technologies make possible social developments that cannot even be predicted today. It is obvious, however, that they will transform the production system. After a wave of automation began to wash through German enterprises, from the second half of 1982 to the first quarter of 1984, productivity rose from 1.5 percent to 10.8 percent in the affected sectors. Employment declined correspondingly, and mass unemployment, along with economic growth, resulted. Microchips are a new universal technology; the possibilities for their application are found in all areas of society. At the same time, however, they embody a technology that creates *possibilities* for restructuring, not constraints; a technology that therefore refutes technological determinism *technologically*.

Sooner or later, the introduction of new media will fundamentally change communication and ways of living and working together for people both inside and outside the workplace. The scope of the opportunities for development is unimaginable. Completely new types of centralization and *de*centralization of the information and production systems are equally possible. The factors that have in the past always led to larger organizations and the growth of bureaucracy are no longer dominant, and may even disappear. Organizational units may soon "cooperate" decentrally, diffused in space. Tasks will probably be outsourced from the production center and processed in new forms of "electronic cottage labor." Entire segments of large organizations can be automated, "delegated technologically" to databases, online information retrieval services, automated customer service, as is already the case with word processors and automatic teller machines).

None of us knows where the road goes or what continually renewed waves of computerization (with unknown effects and side effects) will face us. One important reason for this is that the microelectronics revolution is still in its infancy and continually revolutionizes itself. Nevertheless, we can say today that the scope and depth of these impending changes in industrial society will far overshadow all the decisions made in the political system over the past two or three decades. If knowledge and productive forces continue their explosive development, then one new surge of technological modernization after another will revolutionize the relations of production. It is precisely in its *continuity* with prior development, therefore, that we produce a *new* society (with no awareness of an underlying plan). Paradoxically, the more emphatically we defend industrial society in its conventional forms and cling to its developmental principles, the faster this happens.

IS THE NUCLEAR FAMILY PART OF A FADING ERA?

The nuclear family, which came to dominate in industrial society and constituted its internal social structure, has changed rapidly over the past two decades. The same dynamic that undermined the status-based structures of social classes is crossing over into the family and bringing about a pluralization of family forms: childless marriage, temporary and unofficial marriage, parenthood late or delayed, perhaps even until retirement; in the future there may even be professional parenthood, that is, parenthood limited to a small number of families, whose main function will consist in raising children.

We already have family communes, senior communes, and family units consisting of a single unmarried adult and one or more children. These adults need not be women. In some German cities, it is already possible for unmarried men to adopt children. A new type of "extended family," in which children have multiple parents, is proliferating as a consequence of the increasing frequency of divorce. These are loose "family-spanning familial relations,' more or less conflict laden, between divorced and remarried couples, in which children may have two, three, or four fathers and mothers over time and must find their own way in the chaos.

On the average, every third marriage entered into today will end in divorce. This is how serial marriages come about, that is to say, marriages in succession, which have already replaced monogamy by a series of monogamies. The official divorce statistics only imperfectly reflect the actual number of separations, since there are more and more unofficial marriages that do not require formal and officially registered divorces when they break up. The result is a plurality of life forms, paths, relationships, and wrong turns that can no more be encompassed within the concept of the nuclear family than one can capture a hill of ants with a butterfly net.

In addition, the modernization process is beginning to gnaw "from below" at the biological foundations of parenthood. It may soon be taken for granted that parents can choose the gender of their child in advance, perhaps even its IQ, appearance, or character traits. Embryo transplants, babies from a test tube, a pill that allows one to give birth to twins or triplets, or the purchase of deep-frozen embryos in the appropriate "embryo store"—all these things may seem like fiction, but, at least in initial stages, they are already possible. If babies can be produced in vitro, how does one formulate the concept of motherhood? What consequences will this have for the self-concept of women, who have conceived of motherhood as part of their existence for as long as we can know? Who—or what—is to be designated as the parent under these circumstances? Suppose one woman, for instance, carries to term an embryo that was conceived by another woman. Which of these do we call the mother? Who is considered the father? If a couple can purchase an embryo, will parenthood then become a purely juridical phenomenon?

No matter how we stand ethically on these possibilities, and for the majority of people they will seem like horror stories, this much is certain: if we continue to adhere to the maxims of modernity, then sooner or later these possibilities will be scientifically worked out and implemented. The very adherence to modernity will wash all our concepts of parenthood, motherhood, and fatherhood, as well as our orthodox concepts of the nuclear family, down the river of history. And again, the more emphatically we cling to the status quo and continue in the clear conscience of the nineteenth century, that much more rapidly and completely will we lose the familiar social forms and false a prioris of industrial society.

THE FIEFDOMS OF THE NATION-STATES

We eat spinach from Canada and oranges from Greece. Every evening the world meets at the "village green" of television and exchanges the professionally and politically selected news items—isolated and yet somehow connected. Fashions in clothing, hair, and lifestyles are no longer determined by national borders. Blue jeans, Coca-Cola, and the newest hits from the recording industry—individualized *and* standardized, isolated *and* uniform—are consumed by the world community from San Francisco and Istanbul to Bamberg, even Bamberg. They are on the road to a cosmopolitan exchange that reflects the generalization of technical and methodological knowledge. Nor does pollution recognize any municipal, county, or national boundaries. It streams, flows, and blows wherever it wants. Individual industrial states, developed or not, become dependent, like medieval fiefdoms, relegated to the roles of "national factors" in the calculations of global economic interdependence. They have scarcely any control over the dependencies that grow together through them. The same applies to the military blocs and the pressures to surmount nationality that grew out of them. All of this is tantamount to cancelling the equation of industrial society and the nation-state. We are already in the initial stages of a global social culture and economy with pseudo-independent regional governments. The democratic electoral structure, organized on the basis of a nation-state, does not reflect these global dependencies.

Industrial society, as it developed during the past two centuries in Europe and the United States, is being melted down and recast by the dynamics that it itself continually unleashes through the cumulative effect of new technologies with unforeseeable consequences and opportunities; of internal sociocultural differentiation, pluralization, and individualization processes; and of global cultural, economic, power, and military interdependencies. This metamorphosis of history is occurring as part of the continuity of modernity. It occurs sub-politically, not as the consequence of elections, political revolt, or political revolution, but simply because everything goes on as before. In the developed democracies of the West, which base their self-concept on popular participation in the vital decisions of the nation, a new society is coming into being, unplanned, without a political will, expending all its strength in the constant struggle to avoid the worst.

POLITICAL SCHIZOPHRENIA

Modernity changes and revolutionizes its forms and foundations in industrial society. The absurdities, contradictions, and paradoxes that accompany this "self-historicization" are now bursting into the open. The market, business, and science can only flourish if every certainty, everything ossified, reverential, and moral that blocks their path, is questioned, worn down, and overcome. The unleashed dynamic of modernization is not limitable and not predictable; it can discharge itself gradually and insidiously, and then again violently and abruptly. And yet, the illimitable and incalculable is supposed to run in definite paths, to obey definite premises, to be calculable. Hence, in modernization everything that is predefined and ascribed is cast into doubt, unmasked, and reformed—everything *except* the premises and general conditions of the modernization process itself. People want permanent change, they want the unthinkable to be thinkable, the undoable to be doable, but only with prior reservations and along familiar paths, conventions, and routines. This is a fundamental contradiction in modernity's systematic innovation, which can no longer be ignored. Under these conditions, any action in a principled sense becomes ambiguous and "ambi-ethical," and political schizophrenia becomes the normal condition.

Traditions and traditional social forms are scarcities in the systematic innovation that is subverting them. They are picked apart with one hand and upheld and coddled with the other. Indeed, the emotionalization and ideologization of social forms—class, occupation, family—indicate that their social effectiveness and compelling force are being weakened. Conversely, it becomes possible to institutionalize their opposites, drawing borders and erecting taboos. A society based on innovation needs dogmas and "manufactured" certainties in order to be able to delimit itself and to set itself off from such dogmas by "modernizing" them. The defenders of the status quo in a system based on innovation are also revolutionaries, whether they want it and know it or not. "Conservatives by will" become "revolutionaries of the deed" under the influence of the system. Words and deeds separate and march in opposite directions.

This schizophrenia, in which the left hand no longer knows (and no longer wishes to know) what the right hand is doing, shows up everywhere. People stimulate the economy with new communication media, all the while lamenting that "family values" no longer mean anything. Good Marxists emphasize the anarchy of the capitalist mode of production, but consider it impossible that the classes themselves could be ground up in this anarchic developmental dynamics. Scientists are the real taboo breakers—but God forbid that they themselves should burn in the fire of the questions that they set everywhere; then they see the world ending in a conflagration of irrationalism!

"HELPLESSNESS INTERNATIONAL"

Contradictions of this type and the deep shocks they provoke are the proper "modelling clay" for the most varied and antagonistic political interests and movements. This decade is becoming as indeterminate and as open as a blank page, on which any number of things can be written, painted, or scribbled. The sources of the certainties that supported modernity are beginning to dry up. Behind the façades of routine, helplessness reigns. Helplessness is the real revelation of our times. Now that our optimistic hope of salvation through progress is continually undermined by progress itself (considering our self-created potential for our own destruction and the destruction of nature), now that the intellectual brilliance of a culturally critical cynicism has faded away or, worse yet, become humdrum reality, there is a new, secret consensus beyond agreement contradiction, or cynicism: helplessness.

Helplessness is both the main and the auxiliary speaker at all party conventions. It holds chairs in universities in a variety of disciplinary costumes and routines, in one research institution after the other. It puts on industrious airs, can always be denied, and is never at a loss for an argument. Its favorite diagnosis is paradoxes; its favorite argument is methodologically perfect data production that drowns all questions. A dictate of particular helplessness is the demand for a new ethics that is supposed to overcome helplessness. Helplessness is the underlying patron and author of all the new artistic styles, which confirm and reaffirm their creativity in forms that are admittedly somewhat more tired, more shopworn, not to say, helpless. In social theory, helplessness is easy to recognize: it carries the prefix "post" like a blind man's cane: postindustrialism, postmodernism, postmaterialism, and so forth.

This new international consensus of helplessness has also stolen into the final, impregnable fort of certainty, business. What entrepreneur can honestly open up new markets for his capital by further developing the chemical industry and at the same time be completely, honestly sure that he will not some day place his life's work in the hands of a grandchild who is disfigured down to the chromosome level by industrial toxins? What will happen, to use a familiar and relatively harmless early incident, when the thalidomide babies take over the thalidomide industry? What trade-union official does not know that the strike that he must lead in order to protect the position of the workers and the union is advancing the microelectronics revolution, which will fundamentally change the workers' position and endanger his own? What Green is really free of the suspicion that his battle against the industrial system might also produce mass unemployment, along with all its predictable consequences for those whose livelihood is threatened and for the political system?

Helplessness, which has become a mass movement, a unity party spanning all special interests, the background theory of science, and the dominant practical and academic philosophy, is grounded in the aging of modernity itself. Where tradition has been eaten away, modernity begins to become its own tradition, against which it must demarcate itself and which it must dissolve and rid of dogma. Modernity is shedding its skin like a snake; or, to use a different analogy, it is breaking up its certainties, its coordinate system, and its self-proclaimed eternal truths, just as it broke up the feudal and status-based forms of dominance and production in the nineteenth century and carved out the face of industrial society. Helplessness is the intermediate result of self-disenchantment, in which modernity discovers that its ertswhile self-concept was "naiveté," which must now be overcome. In the continuity of modernity, therefore, there arises a different modernity, a new social form.

The Separation of Modernity and Industrial Society

Classical social theorists took it for granted that modernization was the fusion of the capitalist industrial developmental dynamic with the social and political forms of bourgeois society. It seemed that this symbiosis could be sundered only through a political revolution in which the class struggle dictated by the system would finally reach the boiling point. No one would have believed that industrial society could leave the world stage by the back stairs of history, without any conscious, politically planned, forced revolution. Today, by contrast, it is apparent that the seeming unity of industrial society and modernity is only a historical symbiosis whose own dynamics destroy it. Modernization bursts the categories and the paths of industrial society that it itself created.

In retrospect, one can see that the conviction that modernization was proceeding along the paths and categories of bourgeois industrial society was historical naiveté. Modernization's characteristic trait is that it overruns and breaks up everything; why, of all things, should it proceed for all time *in* and not *against* the social forms and paths in which it originated? How could one assume that where everything changes—family, occupation, wage labor, class, stratum, sex roles, science—the essential things would remain unchanged: family, occupation, wage labor, class, stratum, sex roles, science? How was it possible to conceive of modernity both as a "white heat" in which everything melts away and as an "ice pack" in which everything is frozen solid? Did not modernity introduce itself as a radicalization of historicism? And yet it was presented—for better or for worse—as the *final* industrial society.

Today, by contrast, we are beginning to recognize that the dynamics of modernity break up or recast the social forms of industrial society and to understand how this occurs. The concepts and formulas of class, family, occupation, marriage, female role, male role, sexuality, and love are no longer accurate. Social classes, which still determined the thoughts and actions of people in the first half of the twentieth century, have become dilluted; their status-based inner reality has receded into the background. Each of us, even if we live in a family, lives in a different family. The family has evaporated into famil*ies*, into separate familial worlds. The traditional, unified family situation, once buttressed materially (through scarcity) and normatively, has been replaced by a variety of different, often conflicting situations, roles, and life paths for men, women, and children. These new roles bring with them constant processes of clarification, adjustment, and negotiation. Furthermore, the limits and objectives of familial intimacy, and the satisfaction that this intimacy produces, no longer clearly coincide with the nuclear family; instead, they intersect with and overlap it.

The tendency to cling to conceptual and social forms seems to increase, rather than diminish, with the disappearance of the realities for which they once stood; where reality fragments into subforms and subsubforms, the name finally becomes the only element common to *all* the forms, and it must be defended. Oddly enough, empirical sociology (which conducts research in the *old* forms, and "captures" the deviations in reality with "more sophisticated" methodological refinements) and official social and economic statistics all directly contribute to this. They all see reality slip through the fingers of their conceptual hands. Reality and wish mix and produce a mish-mash that nasty tongues—justifiably—call "ideology."

THE APRIORISTIC NARROW-MINDEDNESS OF SCIENCE AND POLITICS

If one assumes that technological and social innovation will continue forever, then resistance, risk, and follow-on problems arise. That is why primary modernization largely stabilized itself in the treatment of self-produced mistakes and risks. The follow-on problems, which result from new technologies, are defused by making a virtue of necessity: the old technologies are improved, which means that the problems are transformed into new opportunities for technological development.

This model of the market-expanding treatment of technological mistakes is obviously tied to a certain developmental state of the productive forces. Where technical know-how has enabled people to blow themselves to bits, poison themselves, or destroy the natural environment, this trial-and-error method is tantamount to a game of chance involving the suicide of the human race.

And here is precisely where there is another naiveté that is undermined in the internal dynamic of modernity. The development of productivity creates greater and greater possibilities for self-endangerment, which are at the same time less and less amenable to the bandages and ointments from the medicine chest of early modernization. In the waves of modernization that face us, applying this trial-and-error method ("let's just try it—it can always be corrected later on, after all") eventually results in the absurd idea that we can "renew" the dead forest or "heal" the nuclear contamination of whole regions. Language fails: either it goes nowhere, or it objectifies what cannot be objectified. Even trying to formulate the problems is equivalent to trying to explain how a diesel engine works in the language of a pre-technological people. The words used to describe modernity haven't changed, but behind the façade of unchanged words, which have become meaningless, or, worse, cynical and misanthropic in their pseudo-objectivity, there lies hidden the *historical rupture between the modernization of the nineteenth century and the modernization at the threshold of the twenty-first century.* The controversy over science and expert rationality overlooks this, and so is committing a historical category error: it confuses the functions of science in the nineteenth and at the threshold of the twenty-first centuries, or, to put it paradoxically, it confuses one kind of modernization with another.

For example, the Jeremiads on the "health hazards" of a steam locomotive racing along at sixteen miles per hour, or the critique of the natural destruction caused by the development of the modern transportation system, were the kind of shallow critique of civilization that always accompanied modernity but that stimulated it rather than stopped it. The same kind of critique, however, becomes unintelligible and irresponsible when science is playing around with nuclear fission or the genetic code.

It is no coincidence that the images from Hiroshima bring to mind the pictures from the concentration camps after the end of World War II. Science is no longer merely a standard-bearer of enlightenment; it has also become a potential cause of civilization-induced mass immiseration. The crises of the past and the suffering associated with them are no more than a forestaste of the hells we could slide into as unforeseen side effects of the wide-eyed search for knowledge. This is not an ethical problem, nor is it one to be considered at leisure. It is not a problem for scientists to talk over after work, sitting around a festive table drinking wine and racking their brains over whether and how some code of honor can prevent (or perhaps not prevent) the consequences of their global, competition-related praxis in advance (or in retrospect—just which is never totally clear). At stake is one crystal-clear fact (which really ought to dawn on people who have spent any time in the university milieu): twist and turn it as you will, the method of subsequent amelioration, which has tied the market and progress to one another, no longer works. One mistake is two too many. Subsequent amelioration becomes a kind of celestial project, a pact with the afterlife. In the best case it will happen in heaven; but it will probably happen in the hell of earth.

This *new ambiguity* is what we must understand. Under the conditions of the overdeveloped productive forces at the turn of the twenty-first century, science is often enlightenment *and* anti-enlightenment, truth *and* concealment, liberation from inherited constraints *and* confinement in self-created objective constraints. Advocates and critics of science constantly attack each other with one or the other of these two sides. One can continue that way for a long time; and yet both types of justification, taken by themselves, are false. We have to understand that it doesn't work with *or* without science.

The way out of this Catch-22 of contradictions and consequences that the sciences have fallen into since their transformation from productive to destructive forces lies in *considering variable what has so far been considered constant: the sciences themselves*, in their methodological self-image and their division-of-labor and institutional structures. Only one who can see and remove the beam of irrationality in the eye of science can oppose the mote of irrationality in the eye of the critics of science. Just what is "irrational" anyway? Protesting against the devastation of the environment or the risks of nuclear power or the manipulation of human genetics? Or, with the unbroken naiveté of nineteenth-century science, dismissing such protesters as anti-civilization Cassandras?

Science's most resolute defenders and its most radical opponents agree that it has found its ultimate form. There is, therefore, something heretical in the concept of an alternative science, an alternative technology, an alternative knowledge practice (not an alternative theory—those we have in abundance). It blurts out what all honest science already knows but can never admit for reasons of monopolistic self-preservation (even though it is by now common knowledge) that science is a damned earthly business, which has about as much to do with immaculate conception and ascension into heaven as a Stealth Bomber has with a nightingale. Where science is good it is created in bed, like all other good things. Most of the time, however, it has more in common with assembly-line work and with missing the forest for the trees than with knowledge. All that that means here is: an alternative science is always possible.

Furthermore, it may be that, until now, people could be permitted to consider science eternally invariant and to regretfully pass its side effects off as self-created strokes of fate that just had to be accepted. But from now on, this is bad for business, because the destructive and productive forces are interwoven. Science and scientific civilization must change themselves in order to expand and even survive. Just as in the nineteenth century people had to learn, on pain of economic ruin, to adapt to the constraints of wage labor, now and in the future the sciences will have to learn, on pain of physical demise, to conduct an alternative type of science, one that abjures the method of subsequent amelioration and that makes consequences and risks a major consideration in its work.

The historical foundations of the sciences have in fact begun to shift. The primary modernization of the nineteenth century occurred in the *naive objectivization* of possible sources of problems and mistakes. The "guilt" for the diseases, crises, and catastrophes from which people suffered was borne by wild, unexplored nature or the unbroken constraints of tradition. This projection of narrow-mindedness and mistakes into an unexplored no-man's land was tied to a certain developmental stage of modernity—the *confrontation with tradition*. Now, however, in the conditions of *self-confrontation* of modernity, this myth of superiority melts away like reinforced concrete during a catastrophic nuclear accident.

Today, the scientists and the experts are dealing with a world that has already been "disenchanted" and transformed in many ways by science. They no longer encounter "nature" and "traditions" but, rather, fields of action that have already been scientized; that is, the traces, consequences, and problems of past waves of modernization. Gone forever is the power differential of primary modernization, in which scientific experts drove laypeople into clearly delineated and continually shrinking areas, like Indians being pushed back into reservations. Science and technology themselves come into view as causes of mistakes and problems.

But that triggers a movement in which the sciences and the professions have to admit and publicly exhibit their clumsiness, narrow-

mindedness, and defects. The growing risks from modernization ignite forms of alternative science and expert advocates, who now use
the "hocus-pocus of science" in the service of quite different causes,
and who thus reach entirely contradictory conclusions. The equation
of scientific rationality with jurisdictional assignments (certain methods,
theories, or divisions of labor) begins to break up, and new, publicly
oriented forms of expert scientific action arise.

The threats now produced in the modernization process display a
peculiarity not hitherto understood: they are at the same time real
and unreal. On the one hand, many threats and much devastation are
already present in the form of polluted and dying bodies of water,
environmental damage, or new types of diseases of civilization. On the
other hand, we are concerned with projected threats, future threats
which, when they occur, will cause devastation on such a scale that
action taken afterward will be practically pointless. Since these threats
must not be allowed to occur, they create the need for resolute action
to prevent even their possibility or prognosis. The target area of these
threat prognoses no longer lies in the present but in the future. Thereby,
however, the fictitious action-variable of the future becomes a considerable spur to action in social and political conflicts. The consequences
are fundamental, categorical shifts in what is seen as relevant in the
structure of past, present, and future. The past loses its power to determine the present and in its place as a "cause" of current experiences and actions is the future—that is, something *non*existent, contrived,
and fictitious. Let no one be deceived: no matter how farfetched the
self-created threats may seem to be in the midst of flourishing affluence, in the course of modernization they may well undermine the
consensus that has so far supported modernization, bringing about a
power vacuum in the no-man's rule of progress.

SOCIAL THEORY BEYOND "POSTISM"

The changes in science and technology that we have been discussing
must have consequences for social theory and political theory. The
social development of the twentieth century has been conceived of
largely according to the controversies of the nineteenth. Politically,
this meant stirring up or calming the conflict between capital and labor;
theoretically, it resulted in the cognitive and research traditions of
capitalist society and industrial society, which are definitely related to
that conflict. These theoretical and conceptual constructions were extended beyond themselves in the debates of the twentieth century: the
terms "advanced capitalist society," "postindustrial society," and "late-

capitalist society" were coined; however, these only indicate small conceptual "appendices" of the original theoretical conceptions. Thus, labor in "postindustrial society" shifts from the industrial to the service sector, and the development and distribution of knowledge become the central power resources. In "late capitalism" the class antagonisms become blurred, and they are replaced by unstable and elusive "contradictions of the system," which further burden political action and force it to legitimize itself.

As recently as 1968, the controversy over "industrial society" or "late capitalism"—two concepts from the nineteenth century—was still able to bring the Congress of German Sociologists to a boil! Today we notice the *equality* of these "antagonistic" conceptions: both functionalists and Marxists count on the well-worn path of modernization. Even more conspicuous is the extent to which both conceive of the stage modernization has reached as a "*final* situation." There is no transcendence, only "more," "further," and "bigger" along the familiar paths of modernity. The surprising thing is this contradiction: wherever the dynamic of modernization has fully emerged, it is also thought to have halted. In the conceptions of "late capitalist" or "advanced industrial" society, history is thought to have attained both its most dynamic *and* its final condition. It seems to be outside the realm of possibilities that the aprioristic incrustations of industrial society—the compulsory division of labor, commercialization, bureaucratization, the concepts of science and technology—could themselves be caught up in the increasingly heated sub-political dynamic of innovation and be ground up in it, or that the confrontation with traditions could give way to a self-confrontation.

This contradiction shows up in the linguistically and theoretically elaborate "rationalizations" of the belief in progress that functionalism in its various forms has to offer. But it also shows up in the surprisingly explicit way Adorno and Horkheimer promoted the "dialectic of enlightenment" on the one hand while freezing it on the other. The hopes of rationality that informed the beginnings of modernity have been definitely reversed in this "movement of reason." The radicalization of historicization *and* the last days of society coincide. But now it is becoming apparent that modernity is developing a dynamic and projecting risks *from itself* that come into conflict with the nineteenth-century ideas of rationality, social structures, and ways of coping that are traditional to modernity.

The "dialectic of enlightenment" is not the last word. It is already obsolete, and it could only continue after revising its own premises. The same is true of Max Weber's modernization theory or Talcott

Parsons's functionalistically trimmed eschatological optimism. In all of these the cognitive premises and the questions are derived from the historical context of *primary* modernization, which practiced and sharpened its self-image on the basis of its superiority to the mores and traditions it encountered, but which was not yet aware of the problems of a self-modernization of modernity. At the same time, however, a change occurred in the system of reference points that had claimed validity, and that had allowed thought and action to run in dichotomies such as "left" and "right," "progress" and "alienation." Modernity destroys the guiding premises along which it has been conceived.

COLLECTIVE NARCISSISM OR REVIVAL OF THE ENLIGHTENMENT?

There are good reasons to believe that what is often called "*post*enlightenment" or "*post*modernity" (in a delightful, involuntarily frank lack of ideas) not only produces entirely new insecurities and threats but can also be understood as a *revival of the Enlightenment by a radical critique of it*. Such a claim is easy to formulate and difficult to defend; I limit myself to indications here.

The self-historicization of modernity removes the Enlightenment from the historical peculiarities of the nineteenth century that have by now become a prioris. Because the self-produced risks spill over all boundaries, we cannot continue to allow each discipline to be its own sole critic. In interdisciplinary competition and criticism, "side effects" and "risks" blow open the rules for the professional treatment of minor mistakes. New methods of diagnosing and criticizing risks and of setting up and testing hypotheses and theories based on actual effects are becoming established; among them should be the "stress test" of politically motivated public controversies over consequences. Why shouldn't laypeople— who are no longer what they used to be, namely, *just* laypeople, and who ultimately have to pay for all the benefits—ask questions that are forestalled by the false a prioris of scientific theory, and in that way provide a critical supplement to the model of experimental testing? What scientists stigmatize as irrationalism is the revival of Popper's critical model of knowledge, supplemented by the new forum of the "representative public sphere" (consider, for instance, the debate over nuclear energy).

Enlightenment is thus removed from the strictures of the model of science and experts, and in the process, the subject of enlightenment is freed from his heteronomy as a layperson. Or, look at it this way: the laypeople *inside* the experts are beginning to break out of the cage of the unsuccessful self-hypnotic repressions that are conserved and perfected in the expert cultures in which they participate. The lay Indians are rebelling and leaving their reservations. If all goes well, enlightenment is removed a bit from the overprofessionalized approach; it is deprofessionalized and returned to the no-longer-lay people who have managed to demystify the mystery of the demystification performed on them.

The revival of enlightenment by removing it from professional incrustations, however, is only part of the story. Enlightenment has also been rediscovered in a sphere outside the abstract philosophical concern for form and tradition. People have found it on their own, with a casual lack of theory, for home use, one could say, in the catacombs of the subcultures, in the confused relations between the sexes, or in the commitment to resist environmental devastation and threats to peace. "The revival of enlightenment" might seem too grandiose a phrase for such mundane discoveries. But if enlightenment has to do with discovering the constraints in one's circumstances, with opening these constraints up and wresting a bit of a personal life from them, then perhaps these little weeds of self-emancipation, discovered—unsought—and cared for in the garden of one's own life, are the wild predecessors of the hot-house orchid that is usually referred to as "*post-enlightenment.*" No one should try to downplay the fact that people today are dancing around the idol of the golden self, lost in the jungles of a guaranteed self-help industries. But whoever sees only that misunderstands the new element that is *also* turning up here, attempting, hesitantly and off-track, to express itself through unsuitable, worn-out clichés.

Fundamentally, there is something quite banal, simple, and plain here, something one actually dares not say because it has already been said thousands of times, though seldom understood and scarcely ever taken to heart: the plain old insight that human beings can change themselves, not only in such trivialities as life conduct or peculiarities of personality but also in such major things as one's relationship to oneself, to the world, and to reality. Statements like this, however, are always balancing on the knife's edge between being a false pretense to a grand theory, and a glorified platitude.

This needle of enlightenment is found in the haystack of relationships, not under the searchlight of theory; people are pricked by it while groping around for experiences, experiences that, according to prevailing theory, one should not, in fact, *can*not have, but that do exist, in a very concrete, trenchant form—experiences that change society and people's lives from the inside out. We are concerned here, then, with experiences *against* theory, experiences that, must therefore seek and protect their own potential developmental paths.

We are concerned here with something that is the primary and most concrete reality for one person and sheer nonsense for another, which suggests that we are standing on the border between two concepts of experience. For one person, such an explanation can add nothing to personal experience; for another, we are discussing something that doesn't exist, or at least something about which one cannot talk sensibly. Here is the dilemma: in society's subcultures, an experience is spreading and gaining importance—the possibility for taking charge of oneself; for some it is not necessary to speak of this experience, while for others it is *not possible.*

In that sense, Sennett's talk of the "tyranny of intimacies" or Lasch's of the "Age of Narcissism" is correct in some points but is mainly false and misleading. They misunderstand the scope and depth of the unleashed development. Those who judge the new from the position of the old fail to see that here, too, a struggle is emerging for new social ties and solidarities in the family, in work, and in politics. The individualized, detraditionalized lifeworlds have involuntarily entered a historically prescribed experimental phase.

The point is to "experience" new forms of the social that are not determined by the traditional role dictates—man, woman, career, consumption—that are now becoming unreal. At stake is the freedom to express and to follow impulses and wishes that have so far tended to be suppressed. People grant themselves the freedom to enjoy life now, not only in the distant future; to consciously develop and foster a culture of enjoyment; but also to transform personal needs into law and, if need be, to defend them against institutional dictates and obligations. A consciousness of freedom is forming as to how one can defend and protect one's own life against "outside encroachments," how one can have a "space of one's own" (both literally and figuratively), and finally, how one must become socially and politically committed when one personally experiences the endangerment of this free space.

That is why living through experiences in this way also contains the beginning of a new ethic, one that relies on the principle of duty to oneself—not in a solipsistic misunderstanding but, rather, as the expression of an effort to bring the individual and the social back into harmony, in flowing, projective, social identities. Discovering and overcoming the standardizations in one's own life and thought, thinking and living "against the grain of one's own certitudes," become an individual social learning process. The prevailing image of humanity is replaced by an image of humanity that is open and changeable even though it depends upon humanity's changing itself. Humanity's prevailing image of itself, which is built into thought and action and which grows out of social roles and circumstances, is nothing more than a historical hypothesis (and burden), which people have not yet transcended.

The leveled out, untrodden paths that individuals are following here are, in the final analysis, the exact reversal of the steps by which enlightenment has predominately been interpreted and advanced. Progress toward enlightenment no longer follows the succession from a knowledge of nature, through the development of the productive forces, the increase of material wealth, a change in economic, social, and political circumstances, and *then*, finally, to the liberation of humankind. Instead, the end is callously and immodestly anticipated: first the discovery of the self, of its social restrictions and pretensions (and of the practical possibilities of loosening them and breaking them up), and *then* working outward into labor, politics, and institutions as well as into the treatment of nature and technology, by way of marriage, the family, and gender relations. The central problem is always finding and developing the self in the social, and defining the social in a way that will make mutual self-encounter and self-emancipation possible.

MODERNIZATION OF BARBARISM?

To stop here, however, would mean to naively misunderstand the obvious risks of this "exchange of societies." Ignoring civilization's threats to itself for the time being, I see three main dangers in socially and politically overcoming the impending thrusts of modernization.

1. The gap of social inequality is opening again, and radically, to a completely unexpected extent. There are already indications of this development. The continuing waves of microelectronic automation make possible what once appeared impossible: capitalist society is becoming more humane and at the same time more unequal. An organization of labor is emerging in which middle management and routine subtasks in the production sector largely disappear: as their number dwindles, the industrial workers become a new "intelligentsia of production," which overlaps all the previous hierarchical divisions of labor. This implies growing unemployment in an expanding economy and, hence, makes the remaining labor positions more attractive and opens up even better opportunities for their development. The wage laborer who works more independently and with more personal responsibility becomes more important.

By contrast, restrictive routine and assembly-line jobs prove to be just a preliminary to automation. Profits skyrocket rates because of the combination of decreasing labor costs due to automation and increasing productivity: many fewer wage laborers can produce several times as much. As the number of employees decline, companies also save the cost of benefits, which the state cannot replace, in view of its chronically empty coffers. This development, which cannot be overcome by economic growth since that is what produces it, would make it possible to realize the demand for a minimum income decoupled from labor.

2. In the ruins of detraditionalized life forms and lifeworlds, the crisis of identity is spreading like an epidemic. This crisis of identity is not being overcome by a productive turn from the passivity of "one" to the activity of "I"; rather, people become vulnerable to the expansive grasp of flourishing sensation industries, religious movements, and political doctrines. Fun and joy, pain and tears, fantasy, memory, and attention to the moment, hearing, seeing, and feeling all lose their remaining traditional responsibilities for the self and are determined by facts driven by market-expanding fashions. The retreat to inwardness and subjectivity that characterized the 1970s will have pushed barriers aside, contrary to the intentions it was originally based on, in favor of an externally programmed "inward modernization." The tradition of the Enlightenment could receive the final blow in a happy collective brainwashing.

3. What becomes most important politically is the increasing gap between the social and political institutions that arose from industrial society and the society that is moving ever further from the paths and social forms of industrial society. One ends up more and more often with that peculiar phenomenon that Ralf Dahrendorf called the "class struggle without classes" (in a more generalized version, of course). Within themselves, the institutions keep alive an image of social reality that corresponds less and less to external social life. There is something ghostly about political and social conflicts: they take place in reference systems that remind one of the past, like ruins—road markers pointing to nowhere.

NEITHER POSTMODERNITY NOR PREAPOCALYPSE: THE END OF THE NINETEENTH CENTURY

These are extreme scenarios of a possible future; there are other, less extreme, possibilities. And we will have to open ourselves in thought and action to the risk situations produced by civilization and the novel dynamics of social and political conflict contained in them.

The most advanced stage of the development of productive forces sets free the risks of modernization—by which I mean, for instance, radioactivity, which we cannot perceive, but also pollutants and toxic substances in the air, in the water, and in foods, with the associated short- and long-term consequences for plants, animals, and people. These bring about risks that cut across class situation and conflicts. To put it succinctly, *poverty is hierarchical, while smog is democratic.* The social differences and boundaries are relativized by the growth of civilization's risks; privileged ways of living may still provide a refuge from air and noise pollution, but the waters will soon be polluted everywhere, and we will all be equal before more than just the bomb.

This tendency toward globalization is the basis for a peculiar type of distributional logic, the *boomerang effect,* which shatters the class pattern. The risks of modernization sooner or later also catch up with those who produce them or profit from them. The boomerang effect need not manifest itself in direct threats to life; it can also show up indirectly—in monetary and market collapses, in loss of confidence. The destruction of the forest by acid rain wipes out not only entire species of birds but also the economic value of the forest and of land ownership. Contaminated wine not only becomes worthless, but no one even knows where to dump it; worse yet, an entire industry drifts into the margins of existence as companies and jobs are threatened. Here as elsewhere, the principle is the same: property is devalued, *ecologically expropriated.* In these so-far unexplored cases we are dealing with a social and ecological expropriation in which legal ownership is unchanged. And thus the intensification of the risks of modernization creates a genuine and expanding contradiction between the profit and ownership interests that propel the industrialization process forward and its multiple threatening consequences, which also threaten and expropriate property and profits.

At the same time, risks produce new international inequalities, both between the Third World and the industrial states, on the one hand, and among industrial states, on the other. Risks slip under the structure of nation-state jurisdictions. Because of the universality and internationalism of the circulation of pollutants, the life of a blade of grass in the Bavarian forest ultimately depends upon international agreements and their observance. The potential for self-destruction that civilization develops in the modernization process causes the *utopia of a world society* to become a bit more concrete, or at least more urgent. Just as, in the nineteenth century, people had to learn to subject themselves to the conditions of industrial society and wage labor, today they must learn how to sit down together at a table to find and enforce solutions to self-induced risks.

Socially recognized risks—the destruction of forests for instance—contain a peculiar, hard-to-define social explosive. What was hitherto considered unpolitical is becoming political—the elimination of the sources of problems in the industrialization process itself. Suddenly the public sphere and politics are beginning to meddle in the intimate sphere of plant management. Everything is illuminated in the light of a new ecological morality. At the same time, it becomes clear that what is actually at stake in the struggle over defining risks is not only secondary health problems for nature and humankind, but also the direct social, economic, and political effects of these risks: market collapses, capital devaluation, bureaucratic controls, mammoth costs, legal proceedings, votes.

As the threat grows, the old urgencies melt away and there is a parallel growth in opportunities for a centrally planned state-of-emergency policy, which draws its enhanced abilities to intervene from the looming catastrophe. Where danger becomes the normal state of affairs, it becomes permanently institutionalized, and so the risks of modernization also clear the way for a partial redistribution of power, partially maintaining the old responsibilities and partially explicitly altering them.

These are only spotlights on some other new things that must be understood. More than ever, we need new conceptualizations that will allow us to rethink the phenomena that are overrunning us, to live with them and act with them, while still keeping in touch with the positive aspects of tradition and not feeling compelled to sacrifice tradition to a concept of innovation that is itself already antiquated. It is difficult and dangerous to catch the trail of the new concepts that are already beginning to appear today in the collapse of the old dogmas.

Nevertheless, or perhaps for that reason, the world is not perishing just because the world of the nineteenth century is collapsing. The social world of the nineteenth century was never all that stable anyway. It has already perished several times—in thought. In thought, it was actually buried before it was even properly born. It's not just that we are today experiencing a *representative* reenactment, in our living rooms and bedrooms, of the visions of a Nietzsche, or the marriage and family dramas of what is by now "classical" (that is, old) literary modernism. Rather, things thought of long ago are actually happening, with a time lag of roughly a half-century to a century. They have been happening for some time, and they will continue to happen for some time, and they are not yet happening at all.

We are also experiencing, however, what literature didn't show: the fact that *people have to keep on living afterward.* One could say that we are experiencing what happens after the curtain has dropped on an Ibsen drama, the off-stage reality of the post-bourgeois period; or, with respect to the risks of civilization, that we are the heirs of a cultural criticism that has become concrete. Precisely for that reason, we can no longer be satisfied with the diagnosis of cultural criticism, which was always intended to be a kind of admonitory pessimism about the future. It is impossible for an entire era to slide into a space beyond the conventional categories without someone recognizing and discarding that "beyond" for what it really is: the artificially prolonged attempt to reassert control by a past that has seen the present and the future slip away from it.

4

Anthropological Shock: Chernobyl and the Contours of the Risk Society

The following essay was written in May 1986, shortly after the nuclear accident at Chernobyl. It presumes some familiarity with the event and with the public discussion of it in Europe, and particularly within the Federal Republic of Germany. Few media events of the postwar period have so shocked and preoccupied the people of Western Europe as has "Chernobyl," even if this preoccupation has since dwindled and left hardly any or only contradictory traces in everyday political life. I speak of a "media event" because nuclear contamination escapes all perception and turns everyday life into a "political football" for experts and mass media. The confusion was correspondingly complete.

The urgent warning that one should not let one's children play in the sandbox was followed by the unverifiable denial that this recommendation had any validity whatsoever. Those who—"on principle"—consumed eggs and milk only from "well-treated" free-running chickens and cows suddenly ate the products of previously taboo factory-farms and stood in line for dry milk. Meanwhile, however, a freight train with contaminated powdered milk slips through the Federal Republic and confronts politics with simply insoluble problems. The borders between West German states, each of which sets its own levels of acceptable contamination, magically transform the delicacies of one

---

Translated by John Torpey. Special thanks to Christian Joppke.

locality into the intolerable risks of another. To this day, almost all larger daily newspapers carry a column that offers (mostly contradictory) counsels on minimizing the risks through composition of diet: no wonder, then, that Mothers against Nuclear Power have since organized on the national level.

Although the dangers remain invisible, they are extremely effective where they are *believed*: markets collapse and new ones emerge (e.g., a shift from fresh vegetables to frozen). Though they look the same and taste the same, certain products are devalued *tout court* (lettuce and the like). Not only are they impossible to sell; their destruction generates enormous costs. An avalanche of damage claims has been touched off. Entire industrial branches (the atomic and chemical industries) come in for public pillorying.

All this takes place downright mysteriously, since nothing has changed for the eyes, nose, mouth, and hands. It is not only—and perhaps not even most importantly—the fear of health consequences, but also the experience of a *cultural blinding* that makes comprehensible the deep uncertainty that has gripped people since Chernobyl and which still has not subsided. That, in any case, is the argument of this essay. The foundations of life have changed, even if everything appears to have remained the same. The "iron cage," which according to Max Weber was also brought about by modernity, can be felt in yet a different way.

This essay, which was written for the broadly intellectual readership of the journal *Merkur*, attempts to characterize and to comprehend this transformation of consciousness in sociological terms. For the American reader, to whom much of the translated version will sound "typically German," I would add a personal note. Chernobyl affected and influenced me in a very particular way. The event occurred between the submission and appearance of a book with the title *Risikogesellschaft* (*Risk Society*),[1] which I had begun two years earlier. Whereas the phrase elicited only frowns before Chernobyl, it is now on its way to being integrated into everyday speech; the book is in its fourth edition after only nine months. Perhaps this is also a sign of the anthropological shock which I elaborate in this essay.

I

The exception exemplifies the long-repressed rule: everyday life in the nuclear age. The ways in which, in a decisive historical moment, our forms of life have been shattered are to be illuminated here from three sides: the expropriation of our senses; the difference between security and probable security; and the ascriptive quality of danger, which transcends all social differentiations and inequalities.

What would have happened if the weather services had failed, if the mass media had remained silent, if the experts had not quarreled with one another? No one would have noticed a thing. We look, we listen further, but the normality of our sensual perception deceives. In the face of this danger, our senses fail us. All of us—an entire culture—were blinded even as we saw. We experienced a world, unchanged for our senses, behind which a hidden contamination and danger occurred that was closed to our view—indeed, to our entire awareness. A doubling of the world takes place in the nuclear age. The threat of the world behind the world remains completely inaccessible to our senses. This is also true when the degree of contamination is "not hazardous." The global character of the threat and the devaluation of our senses lend to the debate over the degree and dangerousness of the contamination, which now rages in the public and which has strayed into the magical realm of physical formulae, its deep cultural significance.

From one day to the next, Chernobyl made conscious what has already been true for a long time: not just in the nuclear age, but with the industrial universalization of chemical poisons in the air, the water, and foodstuffs as well, our relation to reality has been fundamentally transformed. To use a famous analogy, private control over the means of perception has been overthrown. The senses have been expropriated—in all the splendor of their images of reality. For us, things are no different than they are for heads of lettuce. Thus, just as the lettuce (green, fresh, and crisp as ever), which is contaminated or is considered as such (the difference becomes irrelevant), withers economically and socially in the hands of its owner, our senses have become useless in the face of the atomic danger. It is only too easy and too desirable to deceive ourselves about this by considering only their perfectly adequate functioning.

From another angle, this means that the reality of the danger is always and necessarily administered in a centralized fashion. We are at the mercy of social institutions: weather services, mass media, cabinet offices, officially determined tolerance levels, etc. No mass media information, no consciousness of risk. The physical objectivity of danger and destruction is one issue (a nuclear power plant is by no means only a social definition, but a very real thing). Another aspect is the construction of danger by the social agencies that possess a monopoly in this respect (engineering sciences, legal system, etc.). Finally, everyday knowledge about the danger, which in decisive respects is a sort of fourth-hand knowledge, in others is based on personal evidence opposed to scientific and legal definitions. All three factors vary independently of one another. It is thus hardly surprising that the extremes lie close to each other. Periods of radical unrest follow times of aggressive calm. Both reactions may have the same cause: the unthinkableness of a danger with which one must nonetheless live.

To return to the analogy, the struggle over the means of production has persisted for more than a century, and this conflict still divides the world into political, economic, and military blocs. This comparison is inappropriate in the sense that the struggle concerning private control over perception has yet to begin. Nowhere has that struggle been a theme; it can be found in no party platform, has no parliamentary history behind or before it. Accordingly, this overthrow has taken place more decisively and more quickly. In matters of risk, we *have been* disenfranchised. In nuclear democracy, we the citizens have lost sovereignty over our senses and thus the residual sovereignty over our judgment. This revolution in political, technological, and everyday affairs has been achieved on the quiet basis of normality. Chernobyl created an awareness of it, though only gradually, but it remains always in effect.

A transformation of our way of life has taken place in the guise of undiscussed latent side effects. With respect to nuclear and chemical risk, we have been reduced to media products (insofar as we had not already been so) in the bright glare of our education or ignorance. The disempowerment of our senses forces us into a situation in which we must accept the dictation of centralized information which can at best be relativized in the interplay of contradictions. Even this is of little use, since it only brings to consciousness the generalized lack of knowledge in the face of the danger and the extent to which we are at its mercy.

Parallel with the loss of sovereignty over our senses, a collapse of everyday knowledge has taken place. Our knowledge concerning the aversion of risk, like our entire way of life, is built on the self-sufficiency of our perception—and is correspondingly devalued. This devaluation can be understood in detail. The mass media singled out only symbols: sandboxes, fields, lettuce. In a sense, these symbols took on the function of lightning rods: the concentration of anxiety on them helps to repress the omnipresence of the contamination. And yet there was an "anthropological shock." Without sovereignty over our senses, the dream of privacy is nonexistent. Our notions of individuality, of self-determination, of ones own life, are founded upon personal access to reality. To the extent that we are cut off from this access, we are driven—in the full flower of individualism—into a collective existence at the height of modernity. Of this fact we can deceive ourselves only by refusing to recognize the danger, insisting on the continued functioning of our senses. None are so blind as those who will not see. This adage is true in a revised form: none are so blind to the danger as those who continue to trust their eyes.

II

The atomic danger makes everyday life "headless." No social organs take the place of our senses, however. The nuclear age represents rather the end of perceptiveness and the beginning of a social construction of risk realities. The struggles and strategies over risk definitions are based upon the expropriation of the senses: information equals reality, and thus reality can be created and transformed in the shaping of information and information policy. Nevertheless, one cannot even speak of manipulation: the term derives from another era. Much criticized, advertising becomes *ex post facto* a branch of enlightenment in comparison to the possibilities that develop unnoticed with risk construction. Advertising presupposes adequate sensual self-awareness, which must then be manipulated. These elements recede with the nuclear danger. The construction of risk occurs in the free space of interpretations beyond sensual counter-control. Such constructions, however, are less and less secured through scientific authority and are still bound to the rules of credibility. Herein lies the second part of the shock: those who until now have pretended to know don't know it either. None of us—not even the experts—are experts when it comes to the atomic danger. Here not only individual shortcomings, but also systematic reasons, come to the fore.

It was plain for all to recognize: there is a world of difference between security and probable security. At the same time, the survival of life on earth depends upon this difference. The sciences have *only* the authority of probable security. Their assessment remains true even if tomorrow three or four atomic power plants explode. Until now, we have lived in the false security that probable security meant actual security. Along with this soap bubble, illusions have been punctured about the technical controllability of technical development. In the nuclear age, probabilities of error, even when they attain dimensions that no mathematician would dare to assume, behave in inverse proportion to the survival chances of all. This raises the question how long the development of whole societies will be left to the probability calculations of the engineers.

Now, one might say that the imperceptibility of atomic contamination lightens the burden of everyday life. To be sure, new authority relations arise for the scientifically equipped management of the danger. These relations, however, reduce the already extreme overcomplexity of life. Yet, this assumes stable scientific power to define risks, which systematically has become improbable. The appearance of experts and counter-experts is no accident of the history of science; it is rooted in the very progress and successes of science. With the self-reflection of the sciences, their preconditions and the manipulability of these preconditions become conscious. Refutations become valuable and increase, and with them grows the uncertainty to which science gives rise in relation to the outside world, and which cannot be quelled in the face of the generalization of the methodical skepticism to which this uncertainty leads. The creation of uncertainties—criticism, contradictory results, different ways of proceeding—is the path which the sciences have irreversibly trod with their differentiation, self-application, and the scientific investigation of the risks that their technical use creates. Criticisms of science may also be fed from resurgent irrationalisms, however. Nonetheless, one could proceed with these as before. But the fact that this criticism is produced from within and grows with the successes and self-doubting of sciences relativizes and pluralizes the expert constructions of risk, and exposes them to the maelstrom of doubt.

If only that were all. But the falsifications are the rulers of our everyday lives. It is not only the rapidity with which everyday speech has absorbed the tumble of atomic acronyms such as MCA [maximum credible accident], rem, becquerel, etc. This jargon points to a still fully uncomprehended "emergency-scientization" of everyday life. It symbolizes at the same time a reduction of the lifeworld to technique, the extent of which is only exceeded by the emptiness of meaning which thus makes its appearance. The technicians have not concerned themselves with the question of cultural and social consequences. Nor was that their task. The entire world thus lives and thinks in the terms of a language which suggests technical mastery and the economic usefulness of atomic energy—that is, which presupposes possibilities of action that have nothing to do with the contamination of vegetables and milk, and which have been placed in question before the whole world as a result of Chernobyl, to which this jargon owes its triumph. The bastions of rationality in which the technical sciences used to operate are collapsing—but we are moving in, we must live in them.

III

All this interprets the shock in only a limited fashion. The shock begins to become somewhat comprehensible if one considers the tremors with which all of our constructions of limits, of protected areas, and of possibilities of withdrawal collapsed like a house of cards. Certain unauthorized tongues still speak of the "Communist reactor." The attempt to force together technology and political ideology distorts the lesson of the experience into its exact opposite. Privation, violence, and misery were and are selective. These bring the social hierarchy to bear on the situation and thus presume their opposite: boundaries of unaffectedness, of wealth, of executive power. All of this is no longer true for the atomic danger. It is unselective, global, knows none of the distinctions which our world has thus far constructed: Communists and capitalists, women and men, poor and rich, and oppositions between cultures, nations, and military blocs. Its universalism makes use of a peculiar mixture of nature and society—contamination—and its regime proceeds ascriptively, so that all our concepts of power—action, steering, decision—collapse. This helplessness is symbolized by the generalized staring at the atomic cloud. Two military blocs confront each other. Borders are secured by the most modern armies. And above all of this, moved by the fate of the wind, hovers the cloud, this peculiar, paradoxical combination of weather and history, which transports atomic contamination *gratis* to all corners of Europe.

A fate of endangerment has arisen in modernity, a sort of counter-modernity, which transcends all our concepts of space, time, and social differentiation. What yesterday was still far away will be found today and in the future at the front door. Chernobyl, for instance. Causality can extend over decades. The effects manifest themselves globally, but delayed in time—indeed, only in the struggle over statistical significance or behind the smokescreen of isolation. National states, to be sure, may organize their own decisions concerning technical-economic development either privately or governmentally. As to the consequences of these decisions—and thus in regard to the security and health of their citizens—they have forfeited their competence in the nuclear age. Those who still speak of the internal affairs of another country continue to think in categories that no longer comprehend our reality.

The essence of the matter is that with respect to situations of atomic danger, there are no longer any "others" behind whom one can hide one's own apathy. (Apathy arises here as well. But it has an aggressive impulse, it is an answer, and it must be shielded by new and perhaps even shinier armaments.) Mothers, for instance—formerly *the* unpolitical protectrixes of life in the remaining protective areas of privacy—are now especially among the affected. Their children are in danger. The most intimate—say, nursing a child—and the most distant, most general—say, a reactor accident in the Ukraine, energy politics—are now suddenly directly connected. Perhaps precisely for that reason, this connection may also (have to) be forgotten again. But the rupture within the system of responsibility characteristic of the division of labor until now has been demonstrably completed. The reversal of previous guiding cultural principles manifests itself in the fissures which normality has suffered. In the risk society, of which we are now becoming aware, one must unlearn to trust one's senses and the taken-for-granted; one must learn to mistrust one's senses in order to survive. As an overall cultural situation, this approaches a lab experiment with constantly contradictory stimulus-reaction processes. Whoever uses the loophole of their unchanged perception will find themselves suddenly thrown into conflicts of belief that simply cannot be smoothed out with the means available in everyday life. Everyday and political rigidifications and fanaticizations proliferate in the contradiction between survival and the perception of dangers. The most extreme positions are adopted: some refuse to perceive the dangers at all, while others energetically insist on blanket condemnations in the name of self-protection or the preservation of life on this earth.

IV

In the risk society, the contours of which become apparent here, entirely new challenges to democracy arise. This society contains a tendency toward a "legitimate" totalitarianism of risk avoidance—from below as well as from above. With the rationale of avoiding the one worst-case scenario, the other, still worse, case is created in all too familiar fashion. The necessary debate over the political alternatives of technical-economic development in the age of nuclear fission, of the universalization of chemical poisons, and of genetic manipulation is carried on with too much concentration on the forefront of changing technologies. The question is no longer nuclear power and all the rest, but rather how a bit more social sovereignty can be gained over the society that arises from economically steered technological development. The question is how the power structures and decision rules of technical-economic development, which have forfeited their capacity for achieving consensus, can be refashioned for the epoch of technically mediated social transformation in which we live.

This crucial social-political question, which is gradually emerging from the conflicts over the spectrum of new technologies, is blocked, however, by a discussion of false alternatives. The "philosophy" of "business as usual" (i.e., *back* to industrial society!) is contrasted with the demand of democratizing technical-economic development, the one trying to cancel out the other, while both remain bound to another, bygone epoch.

The politics of reindustrialization, which enjoy great popularity well beyond the trenches of the political parties, lead directly to a staging and a perfection of symbolic, cosmetic forms of intercourse, with risks for which there are a great number of possibilities in the perception-free space of construction. In Chernobyl was an example of unsuccessful information policy, I dread to think of the risk-management of a successful information policy. "Safe" tolerance levels can be agreed upon. This, of course, tends to obliterate their socially constructed character; their "we don't know either" quality was at least apparent when the official levels were different from one place to another. Safety levels can be set high, thus transforming increasing contamination into normality. What does "dangerous" mean, anyway? There are no dead, no injured (in Central Europe). "But there's always been 'natural' contamination, so there is no contamination." Under conditions of higher levels of "normal" contamination, hazardousness is a question of definition which becomes a central aspect of a symbolic non-mastery of the dangers. And this non-mastery takes place precisely where everything else seems to escape political intervention, and the contamination grows by leaps and bounds.

At first glance, such a politics, which replaces action with semantics, finds several conditions which support it. The knowledge of the dangers, which in any case contradicts one's own perceptions, becomes intolerable with the growth and the inescapability of the dangers. In the end, no one wants to know about things they cannot change and which turn their way of life upside down. Precisely because the risks begin to dawn on us in everyday life, the social and political threat arises that those who point out the risks will be condemned as the real danger. But this alliance between the imperceptibility of the threats and their inescapability is extremely unstable. The soft spot of risk societies is their uncertainty about progress. Anxiety rages behind the façade of forced certainties and may reinvigorate all too quickly the old-new specter of blind radicalism. The yearning for a strong hand grows in proportion to the sense that one's world is falling apart. A slick information policy, however skilfully it may employ the theatricalities of "parameters of success" ("control" of sulfur dioxide emissions with simultaneous inattention to many other poisons), threatens with its successes to flip over into its opposite: not the calming of society but rather making it less secure.

The extension of the social-welfare state serves as the model for the counter-demand for democratization. In rough terms, the case is argued on the analogy with the struggle against poverty in the nineteenth and early twentieth centuries. As the extension of the welfare state in Western Europe shows, refusal is not the only option in the face of problems created by industrialism. Instead, such problems can be reformulated in terms of the extension of political action and democratic rights. Accordingly, variations on the theme of an ecological welfare state are brought into play. The argument is that such a state is capable of answering two fundamental problems—natural destruction and mass unemployment.

Without wanting to criticize these conceptions *in toto*, it must nonetheless be said that this social-political strategy threatens to achieve the opposite of its intentions. In an effort to stem the dangers with which we are confronted, this strategy sees itself forced to erect a network of bureaucratic controls over all realms of everyday life. To categorize, classify and regulate everything in scientific-authoritarian-bureaucratic fashion belongs to the false logic of risk avoidance. For the sake of protecting the most loved and the most powerless—animal and plant species threatened with extinction, children coughing due to smog—they run the risk of recognizing no mercy. The environmental wisemen [*Umwelt-Weisen*] of the Federal Republic offer a foretaste of things to come in their special report on "The Situation of Agriculture" (Bonn 1985). They call for official "fertilization permits," "binding fertilization plans with concrete specifications concerning the type, extent, and schedule of application," as well as a corresponding differentiated system of "environmental monitoring" and a "revision and further development of the legal framework."

V

We must counterpose a neither/nor and a third option to the either/or of reindustrialization and democratization. Both are premised upon the model of classical industrial society, in which it is assumed that politics has or should have a steering center above and beyond all vicissitudes and differentiations. The argument is that the various threads have to run together in the political system and its democratically legitimated institutions.

But this argument fails to do justice to what I would describe as the unbinding [*Entgrenzung*] of politics. A multifaceted spectrum of mainstream, peripheral, sub-, and counter-politics has arisen in developed modernity with its differentiation, with the achievement of basic constitutional rights, and with the political mobilization of the citizenry. It is not necessary to decide whether it was ever appropriate to conceive of a steering center of modernity which constituted the basis for the specialization of politics in its legally relevant institutions. In any case, with the development of modernity and the achievement of its principles of autonomy, differentiation, and individuation, this conception becomes increasingly inappropriate—and more dangerous. For it suggests failure when in fact the consequences of the claiming of fundamental democratic rights have changed the basic situation of politics and economics, science and technology. This transition from executive politics into a political process, according to this assessment, is not correctible by means of the demand for democratization. To the contrary, all demands for centralization contradict the extent of successful differentiation and democratization of the society.

To put it another way: when everyone awaits the contours of another society not from the legislative debates in parliaments nor from the decisions of the executive, but rather from the application of microelectronics, reactor and genetic technologies, or the transformation of gender relationships in family and occupation; where the parliamentarians pander after the mass media and political decisions are annulled by the courts, it no longer makes sense to locate politics only in the political system. The concept of politics becomes hazy and requires redefinition. This opposition of various decentralized centers of sub-politics—economy, trade unions and employers' organizations, media publics, the family, science, courts, social movements—with very different possibilities for influence, objectives, inertial tendencies, and dependencies, is not only cause for complaint. It is the changed point of departure for a developmental model of differential politics.

Today, monopolies are breaking up that originated with industrial society: the political monopoly of politics, the knowledge monopoly of science, the occupational monopoly of men, the technical-economic organizational monopoly of capitalist firms. Monopolies are breaking up, but no worlds are collapsing. All this is becoming brittle in the same way that the structures of feudal society began to dissolve in the nineteenth century, and for the same yet historically deferred reason: modernization, which now runs up against institutions of industrial society which were only apparently built for all eternity. Something that no one expected and that none of the classical social theories anticipated or even considered is now taking place: de-traditionalization strikes the de-traditionalizers with full force. But this turn of events is not as misguided as it at first appears. It lies rather in the continuity of modernity, whose intrinsic dynamic of dissolution now extends itself to its first social form, industrial society. With it are bound up ambiguous, unforeseeable consequences. Each of the monopolies that is breaking up today stands in contradiction to the principles of modernity. The monopoly of politics has always been based on a partial democracy, leaving social transformation by technology and economy to the blind causality of the market. Science's monopoly of rationality hides the self-doubt that is promoted internally. The occupational monopoly of men stands in contradiction to the universalistic demands for equality under which modernity arose. In other words, many uncertainties and unanswerable questions arise in the achievement of modernity and are deployed to avoid the short-circuiting of their principles in the project of industrial society. The other side of the dangers in risk society is the opportunity to find and to activate that surplus of equality, freedom, and self-determination that modernity promises *against* the limitations, the functional imperatives, and the fatalisms of progress characteristic of industrial society.

What are the consequences of this for a new understanding of politics and sub-politics? A first step in this direction is that politics must overcome the prevailing "as if" and accept the consequences of the self-limitation that has taken place historically. Politics is no longer the only or even the central locus for deciding about the social future. The issue in election campaigns is not to choose a national leader who then controls the instruments of power and who is responsible for everything, both good and bad, that happens during his or her administration. If this were so, we would be living in an elective dictatorship, not in a democracy.

The same is true for another side of the same relationship: the various realms of sub-politics. The economy, science, the family, the public sphere can no longer behave as if they weren't doing what in fact they do—making policy with their particular means. There is nothing indecent about this; it is rather the unveiling and the admission of the possibilities for social change that the development of modernity has revealed in many areas. This opens up the central question of how industrially produced dangers and destruction can be eliminated or reduced under the conditions of differential politics.

My suggestion points in two directions: the autonomy of risk avoidance should be subsumed by the autonomy of sub-politics. In other words, the law of latent side effects, which burdens us with the risks, must be broken by insisting that those who create the risks take responsibility for them. Capitalist firms, for instance, would be confronted with the necessity of demonstrating the harmlessness of their materials and their products before they are introduced into circulation. Hordes of researchers would no longer have to run around trying to guess which work structures and forms of organization might arise in relation to microelectronics. Firms would instead find themselves with the task of researching in advance and of saying how these things are to look, and only then taking up their work. Certain risks would still remain which seem too great in terms of various considerations, and these must be averted. In such cases, state policies must create frameworks for regulation. A variety of means are at its disposal to achieve this end.

The intimate relationship between economics and technology policy is by no means necessary, and it frequently enough undermines the credibility of politics because it falls into the situation of having optimistically to justify that which arises "naturally." In essence, this approach confuses the problems of poverty in nineteenth- and twentieth-century Central Europe with the risks of technological development at the end of the twentieth century. Whereas the struggle against poverty runs into the firm opposition of private investors, which arises from increases in wage and benefit costs, risk definitions *divide* the economic camp. For here there are potential *losers*, to be sure, but potential *winners* as well. Blanket burdens for all fall away, and in this sense risk definitions contain a set of options for a politics that seeks to avert risks at their roots.

But that would only be the half of it. The other half would consist in supporting and extending the counter-control and counter-influence possibilities of sub-politics. Essential in this regard are strong and independent courts, the personnel of which must be openly and pluralistically chosen, and strong and independent media publics. These two central pillars in the system of sub-political counter-control, however, as the past has taught us, are insufficient by themselves. An essential complementary step is necessary. The possibilities of self-control, which all owners of monopolies cherish, must be complemented by possibilities of *self-criticism*. That which until now has only been able to be achieved through laborious struggle against the dominance of professions and company management must be institutionally guaranteed: counter-expertise, intra-professional and intra-company conflicts over self-engendered risks, repressed skepticism. In this instance, Karl Popper is certainly correct: criticism means progress. Only where medicine confronts medicine, atomic physics confronts atomic physics, human genetics confronts human genetics, and information technology confronts information technology can it become externally comprehensible and determinable which genie is in the bottle. The facilitation of self-criticism in all its forms is no hazard, but rather probably the only way to discover in advance the error that could bring the world tumbling down around us. The particular regulations and supports that will promote this self-criticism are not yet apparent. Much would be gained, however, if those regulations were dismantled that make people opinion slaves of those for whom they work. Then it would be possible for technicians to report about their experiences in firms and not to have to forget about the risks that they see and produce when they leave the company gate.

Note

1. Ulrich Beck, *Risikogesellschaft: Auf dem Weg in eine audere Moderne* (Frankfurt a.M., 1986); (English translation *Risk Society: Towards a New Modernity* [London, 1992]). This article presents only one central thesis of the book itself, which elaborates themes of class structure, gender conflict, science, and politics in "risk society."

5

We Fatalists:
In the Labyrinth
of Risk Society

We have been living for a long time now in a consensus that can be hidden only with great difficulty behind all our quarreling and ostentatious activism: the consensus of industrial fatalism. I would like first of all to argue that this consensus is the quintessence of all experience in and with modernity, secondly to refute industrial fatalism, and, thirdly, to see what there is left to do afterwards.

I

The argument is quickly given. If there is anything that unites the contradictions that tear the age apart, it is the conviction that we are stuck in the shell of our dependence on rationality, that our productive forces create a liberation which ends up enslaving us, that we are captives of a rationality that has flipped over into irrationality; or, that we are functional differentiators of such a functional differentiatedness that everything is becoming more functional and more differentiated. These are all variations on the fundamental theme of industrial fatalism, in major or minor key, with celestial or infernal visions, for flute or percussion, from Comte to Adorno, or from Marx to Luhmann.

Walter Benjamin has impressively testified to the fatalism of progress:

There is a picture by Klee entitled *Angelus Novus*. It shows an angel, looking as if he were removing himself from something he is staring at. His eyes are open wide, his mouth is open, and his wings are

77

outstretched. The angel of history must look like this. He has turned
his face to the past. Where a chain of events appears in front of *us*,
he sees only one big disaster, ceaselessly piling rubble upon rubble
and throwing it at his feet. He would like to stay perhaps, awaken
the dead and repair what has been smashed to bits. But a storm is
blowing this way from Paradise that has so caught his wings that he
can no longer close them. This storm pushes him relentlessly into the
future, to which he has his back turned, while the pile of rubble in
front of him grows up into the sky. What we call progress is *this* storm.[1]

The questions and critiques are getting louder, growing into a readiness
to do more than just sign petitions. The word "no" is becoming popular: both the Catholic church and the feminists are demanding it. It is
being considered in Switzerland and in the trade unions. Across political parties, even occasionally in government ministries, discontent
is growing. Motley coalitions are emerging, coalitions that include angry
farmers, critical doctors, genetic technicians, and lawyers. But the process
at issue is occurring like a divine judgment, with what seems to be an
irresistibility beyond "yes" or "no." Commitment shatters on an uncon-
trolled industrial dynamism, whose momentum is only exceeded by its
contradiction of the principles of rationality and democracy that allegedly direct it. When it comes to action, helplessness and hopelessness are the program of the opposition, which enjoys ever greater interest.
When ten counter-examples spring up for every good argument, commitment almost of necessity turns into fatalism.

Assume that the impossible were to become true. Would there not
still be a couple of hundred nuclear power plants on our doorstep in
Europe and the world? Would not curtailing the second Creation—
that is, through genetic technology and commercial eugenics—deprive
our agriculture of its international competitiveness? No sooner does a
group of resolute people unite against experimentation on human
embryos than they hear shouts of "You're preventing life-saving research on AIDS!" And the internal law of uncontrollability is freedom
of research itself, the unpredictability of the consequences of scientific work. Furthermore, doesn't sympathy for millions of unemployed
end up forcing us to once again look the other way? Laws? Don't we
have more than enough of them on the books already? Isn't it true
that the lack of enforcement arising from the power relationships in
the no-man's land of unaccountability already stinks to high heaven,
high hell, or wherever?

Even in the fruitless struggles on the platforms of European politics
over the vitally necessary task of reducing the levels of exposure considered acceptable, for instance, it is demonstrated to us over and over

again how, in the prevailing system, toxins are allowed free passage by international obstacles against a preventive industrial policy. We even manage to transform government inactivity on the international stage into activity: people pride themselves on being in the vanguard.

Instead, the controversies take place in arenas so far from the center that any conflict that might arise can be fought out almost without consequences. The "side effects" of progress not only presume their own causes and causers to be constant, they are also uncertain and unknowable in any case. This must be emphasized. Ethics are to be invoked on Sundays and holidays after the work is done; supporting them seems lucrative simply because their lack of binding force is part of what makes them so compelling and because dramatizing ethics implies dramatizing their antagonisms, in which they perish.

The *courts* impenetrably condense a plain yes to everything new from science, business, and technology into clauses and instances. Cutbacks in auxiliary areas only strengthen the main development. There is no better way to symbolically detoxify a threatening reality, which remains threatening precisely because it is symbolic. The condemnation of accidents, with its concentration on extreme cases, is followed by rituals that threaten to submerge the catastrophic aspects of normality in normality. Things stirred up in the public sphere do not take place only in the isolated semi-irrelevance of the media spectacle, which also follows its own laws: it can be statistically established that the "decay time" of public alarm varies from a couple of weeks to several months, depending on the nature of the disaster.

Social movements, if one takes the term literally, mean coming and going—particularly going. Self-dissolution is their leading characteristic.

We are still puzzling over what happened to the shock and the terror that ripped people out of normalcy after Chernobyl. Perhaps the answer is obvious: perhaps we all awoke one morning as heroes from one of Kafka's novels, arrested by a danger we can never escape by anything we can do.

Life and action in risk society have become Kafkaesque in the strict sense of the word.[2] It begins with the violation of privacy, as in the case of Josef K.—two gentlemen arrest him in his bed. The threats slip under all the barriers and all the constructions of a "personal life" of which we have grown so fond. They are just there, not subject to decision making, unopposable, in the most intimate aspects of life: breathing, eating, playing, nursing children, and so on. The entire canon of our everyday knowledge fails. The instruments of opposition— our senses and our judgment—have been expropriated overnight. Those who distrust their senses, however, are "arrested," suspended on the

puppet strings of centralized information and labyrinthine information administration—mass media, ministries, experts, and the like—
of which one can say with certainty only that they contradict one another
and thus deceive.

The deeper we penetrate into the tangled corridors, rooms, and tunnels
of hazard production and administration, the more obvious it becomes
that we are dealing with a giant bureaucracy that reaches down to the
factory level, a bureaucracy of general carelessness and insecurity, of
growing non- or half-knowledge, of falsification and concealment according to the brilliant organizational principle of unaccountable non-
jurisdiction.[3]

But the entire absurd comedy (Kafka and his friends were unable to
suppress their laughter during readings of his works in small groups)
only becomes apparent when there is protest: without expert judgment,
criticism is empty; with expert judgment, criticism will be refuted. Protest must speak the language of science, which serves both the production of the threats against which people protest and the protest
and opposition to them: protest must adopt the fundamental mistakes
it is attacking before it can even open its mouth. It's like arm-wres-
tling with oneself: A person has to pull himself across the table in
order even to start. What remains after that is playing one science off
against another. The joke is that in order to protest one must argue
even more scientifically than the scientist one is arguing against.

All along the journey through the courts, accordingly, protest en-
counters scientific gatekeepers, whose defense is as clever as it is effective. They greet protest with the charming but ambiguous inquiry into
the precision of its concern (which they know only all too well and
basically share). Then, on the chain of a burden of proof, which it
itself forged, they lead it into the labyrinths of unprovable things that
must be proven. They do not lead it astray, God forbid, into the se-
crets of strict scientific discipline, which protest must make its deepest
concern if it is not to become guilty of pure irrationality. Anyone who
follows this advice and really ponders things can only end up begging
pardon for his impertinent behavior, and must in addition look inside
himself for the cause of the threat-consciousness that tortured him and
urged him on. The result is exaggerated fears, subjective feelings of failure, and concealment of insecurities resulting from unemployment, marriage, and family problems, which are projected onto the surroundings.

The smothering of protest in itself resembles the fate of Josef K.
The absurdity of the punishment—threat—is so incomprehensible, so
unbearable that the accused seeks a justification for the punishment
in himself in order to find peace. Josef K.'s Trial began with subjuga-

tion as the principle of revolt. It ended with the accused making accusations against himself and punishing himself in the service of his accusers. It will probably not be too much longer before the slight increases in birth defects in Germany from Chernobyl, which really cannot be statistically proved anyway, will be ascribed by elaborate studies to the fears stirred up in the mothers—and *only* that, which implies that mothers who believe this need fear only themselves in the future and nothing else.

II

When everything has been said, proven, found disappointing, and refuted, and when everything is threatening—that is when discovery begins. And at the beginning of the discovery is, as usual, one discovery. There are three versions of industrial fatalism: positive, negative, and cynical.

Optimistic (opportunistic?) fatalism, the trust in progress, is certainly still the dominant (I almost said the "healthiest") attitude because it affirms what is happening in any case. That is why it does not exactly give off the odor of freedom. Belief in progress grovels before a throne that can no longer be abolished, whose rule cannot be softened or justified by the exchange or sharing of power, whose power is not even ascribable to a person or institution. So impenetrable is this "no-man's rule" of progress (Hannah Arendt), that apparently only one option remains, consent.[4] A tyrant who cannot be overthrown or voted out *must* be loved. Or hated—but the insight that the power to which one feels subject is inescapable resonates even in the hate.

This wisdom of embracing the inevitable *qua* inevitable refers to and preserves the belief in progress. By accepting the insight that what is happening anyway is progressive, embracing the inevitable cancels out the contradiction between not being able to act because of overwhelming circumstances and yet really having to act in the age of democracy and enlightenment. If people now give in, they give in to the radiant perfection of humanity, and not from naked lack of alternatives. Here and there the strength grows out of this affirmation to cut off or steer away what threatens us as the worst of the worst, or at least to hope for such strength.

The pessimists, the prophets of doom, the negative fatalists, have certainly increased in recent years. Perhaps there has even been a falling away from naive industrial tribal consciousness, from belief in the machine gods of progress. In my own, completely non-binding estimation, the nineteenth-century faction—the staunch optimistic fatalists of progress, waving their flag of the future, whether red or black—is suffering a severe erosion of membership. Many of the deserters, and this is interesting, leap directly from optimism to cynicism, flying right over pessimism.

There are reasons for this. Pessimism is extremely uncomfortable, unlike cynicism, which rejects all value judgments, including negative ones, partly from the realization of their destructibility and decrepitude, and partly from the pragmatism of doing things in this world. It is once again possible to live with a cynical attitude toward progress. This is consent beyond consent (or non-consent). People in the second century of industrialism have cast off both the burden of defending the now-untenable naive industrialism of the early days and the burden of mounting an attack against it. People can lean back; they can even dance on the volcano. Cynicism gives that certain absurd something, the thrill of panic, to the consumption spree of the post-consumption age. Rejection, amplified into the rejection of rejection, forms an almost impenetrable cushion behind which one can enjoy the comfort of consenting to and the advantages of rejecting goals that were probably dominant from the beginning: unconditional consent, in advance, to the way of the world.

By contrast, the pessimists, who see enlightenment as having been dismissed and transformed into its opposite, find themselves sitting in the wrong train, without an engineer, and they can neither get off nor pull the emergency brake. They run to the end of the train and press their noses against the windows. But they're moving! They hammer on the windows. But they're moving! And the train has not yet exploded like a balloon, as, in pursuing their criticisms, they keep predicting, in the face of mocking laughter and in obvious contradiction to the continuing movement. It seems odd that they repeatedly simulate an emergency braking. Because they're moving! And they themselves know they're moving and that nothing they can do, no matter how thoroughly critical or cleverly negative and skilled they are, can stop or divert the motion, not because this is in principle impossible, but because the radical criticism of irresistibility feeds on its object.

The other passengers owe a lot to the small group of critical doubters and despairing critics who do not let themselves slip into cynicism. They are the ones who note the lack of what others no longer dare to notice—brakes, anything resembling a steering wheel, the redemption of the powers that be: democracy, self-determination, enlightenment. With their sad, bitter, angry, and ridiculous gestures, the pessimists are the ones who at least remind their fellow passengers of what is missing.

Beyond all their differences, it is also true that optimism, pessimism, and cynicism are variants of consent to industrial fatalism. There is a growing critique of the belief in progress, of course, but no critique of industrial fatalism. Enlightenment ends in the fatalism of developed industrial society, which, on the one hand, transforms everything into something that can be done and, on the other, sanctifies and blesses its nearly total paralysis of action with the holy water of progress. Protests, no matter how insistent or desperate, only confirm the fundamental theme of irresistibility and irreversibility. This is what gives protest's warnings their siren-like quality. Industrial fatalism is not only not a contrast to a radical critique of progress, it is actually its origin and star witness. Apologizing for progress and criticizing it are the opposing voices in the duet of industrial fatalism.

Contrary to our self-image of the industrial age as being ideologically torn, behind the surface antagonisms we are dealing with a monolithic block of homogeneous basic convictions that is virtually unique in world history, the triplets of industrial fatalism. This only becomes visible in the struggles over the paradoxes of high-industrial threats.

III

What is generally assumed could also be true. Is progress, after all, the disaster that was supposed to be avoided? Don't we need, more than anything else, a utopia in which the inevitable is worthy of affirmation?

Everything has been invoked: reason, ethics commissions, parliaments, the charisma of gifted leaders, the cost explosion, and the collapse of nature. But, despite all the fanfare of decline, these are probably just the alternate band marching along, serving only to accompany the triumphs of industrial development. Industrialism arose against the empty hand of good will, no matter how frequently or powerfully announced, and it is therefore well armored. What occurred to no one was the possibility that the very victory of progress may be what puts the brakes on progress, what tips it over, or at least what makes it look thoroughly questionable. The challenger and refuter of industrial fatalism is—industrial fatalism. Unconsciously, unwittingly, and aimlessly, modernization is undermining itself. In the process, however, restratifications in social structure are developing, along with shifts in power, new lines of conflict, and new possibilities for coalitions. Ethics, the public sphere, mass media, new thinking, social movements, and individual action are all getting their historical chance.

More concretely, it is not the Frankfurt School that refutes the (positivistic) ideal of science, but, rather, the autonomous development of science itself, which does not stop, indeed, cannot stop, its journey along the paths of narrow-minded speculation, even at the risk of demystifying its own foundations and products. Someone who stirs up doubts about his own foundations may find out, if he does a good job, that he no longer has a job. During this century, the very core of science, the experimental support for the natural sciences, has quite simply been thought to bits and doubted out of existence in long, thorough debates that were supposed to decode rationality.

Specialists who intrude into everything shouldn't be surprised if disparate results are proclaimed for all publicly discussed issues, results that often aren't even contradictory because they cannot even be referred to each other. If everything is investigated, even the destructive effects and threatening risks of scientific development, then (involuntarily and unknown to the specialists) the sciences are also, with their inherent thoroughness, refuting their assurances of safety from yesterday and for tomorrow—until finally the public (subservient to science even here) begins to get the creeps.

This all follows from the success of the established claims of science. Ultimately then, doubt conquers knowledge, which owes everything to doubt, and thereby is created another situation, not yet understood, beyond "positivism" and the "Dialectic of Enlightenment." The triumph of scientific rationality turns into a subliminal democratization of the scientific monopoly on knowledge. Scientific arguments are becoming as moldable and mutually relativizable as their objects, and thus people other than scientists can once again have a say.

Similarly, in the era of mega-risks, the era of its greatest successes, technology has also suspended the validity of its procedural logic of learning from its mistakes—surreptitiously and behind the backs of those who conduct the research. Take nuclear energy as an example. Theories about its safety can no longer be tested in the laboratory, but thereby the relation between theory and practice is turned upside down. Practice becomes a laboratory experiment and the public become guinea pigs, part of the experiment.[5] At the same time, research takes place under the Damocles' sword of horrendous investments. That is to say, scientific dogma flourishes in the shadow of mega-risks. Mistakes that cost billions can no longer be admitted.

The law represses reality where it should be serving justice. Thanks to a series of legislative and procedural constructions, the jurist becomes a mere legal adviser for technology. The greater the threat to fundamental rights, the less the legal protection.[6]

Business, seemingly self-assured in blaming the threats it produces on the unaccountability of the surroundings, produces conflicts in its own quarter to the extent that it succeeds. It may even be slipping into a new social structure, with completely unpredictable effects and conflicts, because there is a category error concealed in the talk of "environmental hazards." People speak of the destruction of "nature" and "the environment" at a historical juncture when such things no longer exist. What one party, the chemical industry perhaps, pollutes and calls "the environment" is what others, tourism, fisheries, or agriculture, have for sale on the market.

In the integrated and multiply vulnerable context of nature and society in which we live, destruction of the environment is also destruction of products, property, and market shares, which is an inherent contradiction of industrial society.[7] There is bitter irony in the prevailing attitude of industry: thank God for the environmental movement, which, despite all its political activism, cloaked and mediated in "environmental hazards," still conceals the fact that the conflicts are both aroused and concealed between various factions of capital, between winners and losers of social risk situations and definitions.

IV

If industrial fatalism is true, then it is obsolete. We have taken the liberty of not beating on it here with the club of moral criticism but, rather, of leading it to the historical sidelines on the basis of its own historical truth; the side effects of the side effects add up to a new modernity.

Societies that first conceal and then, during the shock of an industrial disaster, confront the historically new phenomenon of the socially produced but unaccountable possibility of destroying all life, are what I call *risk societies*. The overarching feature of this epoch is not a physical one, the looming destruction, but a social one, the fundamental, almost universal, and scandalous failure of institutions in the face of destruction.[8]

All the risks of the industrial age have associated provisions for *after-care* (fire departments, insurance, psychological or medical care, and so on). In contrast, general consent to the entirely incomparable dangers of risk civilization is expected with no after-care. There are no existing institutions and probably none are conceivable that could be prepared for the "maximum credible accident" (MCA) and could, even in this worst case, guarantee the integrity of the social order, of the cultural and political structures. There are, however, many institutions that are specialized in the only possible response—denying the threats. The dogma of infallibility takes the place of security through after-care, and the keeper of the dogma is the queen of error, science. Only Communist reactors, not Western ones, are empirical creations of human hands, capable of throwing all the scientists' theories overboard. Even the simple question, "But, what if?" exposes the lack of any planning for after-care. Thus, political stability in risk societies is the stability of not thinking about such problems.

Gradually, accident by accident, the logic of the institutionalized neglect of problems is being revealed as illogic. What is the relevance of probabilistic safety prognoses—and thus of the entire analysis of natural science—for the assessment of an MCA, which would destroy life but leave the theories intact?

Sooner or later, the question arises as to the value of a legal system that pursues even the smallest detail of technically manageable minor risks but uses its authority to legalize the mega-risks, unless it can whitewash them technically, and then forces them upon everyone, including the many who resist?

How can belief in economic growth and prosperity survive at the same time that property and the basis for the economic existence of entire industries are being disrupted and destroyed? How can a political authority be upheld that is compelled to counter the escalating consciousness of risk with ever more energetic assertions of safety, but that thereby subjects itself to permanent attack and puts its entire credibility at risk with each accident or sign of an accident?

Industrial disasters are not natural disasters. They are artificial disasters, in which people can no longer summon their creator, God, before the court of enlightenment, as was still possible after the great Lisbon earthquake in 1755. The accused in the disasters awaiting us will be the guarantors of law, order, prosperity, rationality—of democracy itself. The agents of disaster, however, continue to lull themselves in the security of industrial society and its familiar antagonisms. In their industrial torpor they react to the challenges of the nuclear, chemical, and genetic age as if they were in another century. They sit on the high throne of eternal industrial verities, like the feudal lords who condemned and dismissed the growing power of the bourgeoisie and the working classes on the basis of their inherited legal, property, and conceptual systems. By virtue of their institutionally well-developed and oft-praised abilities to define reality itself, they deny the realities that are undermining them.

This is the club of would-be Hegels. People imagine themselves to occupy the peaks of world history. If there is a supreme paradox in this age so rich in paradoxes, one that commands all the other paradoxes, it is that social history, which has finally become autonomous and irresistible, is now being conceived of as static. The future is nothing but the past and the present running in neutral at high rpm.

Hiroshima was terrible, horror plain and simple. There, however, it was still an enemy who attacked. "What would happen if the horror came straight from the center of the productive sphere of society, not the military? What industrial policy would follow the first civilian holocaust? What crises of technology, democracy, reason, society?"[9]

Even if this is only a threat, institutionalized neglect puts the social contract up for grabs.[10] In these conflicts over progress, previous political categorizations and ideological force fields dissolve, and "rainbow coalitions" are forced into existence, coalitions whose members would be arch enemies in industrial society.

It may make sense to differentiate two phases here. There is one in which risk society dictates the problems, but the majority of people and the institutions continue to think according to the categories of industrial society. And there is a second, between psychological repression and hysteria, in which the social mechanism of risk society is recognized and the guiding political problem has become the struggle over the institutions of prevention, accountability, and participation in decision making—the struggle, that is, to overcome the no-man's rule created by industrial society. In this phase, the institutional earthquake made permanent by magnifying the contradictions over unaccountable risk situations enters into consciousness and action.

The phase of risk society politics that is becoming visible today, in the area of disarmament and detente, can no longer be understood or pursued nationally, but only internationally, because the social mechanics of risk situations ignore the nation-state and its alliances. Military and economic constellations that seemed to be cast in concrete are beginning to move, and this also compels, or allows, a new European politics and perhaps corresponding shifts in domestic power and coalitions.

Among the most drastic consequences, however, will probably be significant shifts in the political sphere. While the façades remain intact, power positions—almost like auxiliary governments—are emerging among the risk situations that depend on publicity and definitions—weather bureaus, research laboratories, nuclear power plants, chemical factories, editorial offices, courts of law, and so on. Seemingly self-referential systems are becoming susceptible to action and dependent on individuals. The Davids are getting their chance. The colossal interdependence of the effects of risks—the collapse of markets, property rights, trade-union power, and political responsibility—is creating key positions and media of risk definition that cross the political and professional hierarchy. For instance, someone who managed to rewrite the standards for interpreting causality to apply to the international interchange of pollutants, to pursue a reform of causality, in other words, would have virtually amended the constitution and would create a different republic by that fact alone. For this would bring changes in economic, technical, and legal structures. The fact that the appropriate access and opportunities would have to be forced open, argued for, and legally protected does not contradict this argument; rather, it supports it.

It would be completely wrong, however, to conclude that a new Enlightenment is dawning, dropped into our laps by a charitable History. What is coming into being is not simply "technocracy" or "capitalism" or whatever the other popular buzzwords might be. On the contrary, the perspective suggested here may even remind some of an attempt to bail out the water flooding into a ship at sea by boring a hole in its bottom.

Notes

1. W. Benjamin, *Illuminationen* (Frankfurt a.M., 1980), p. 255.
2. This concept designates the situation of the individual that can be experienced, in reality or in literature, in a totalitarian and labyrinthine world that is incomprehensible to the individual, that cannot be characterized by any other word, and to which neither political science nor sociology nor psychology can provide a key. What Max Weber elaborates as "bureaucratic rule" from the viewpoint of administration, and what Hannah Arendt decodes as the "banality of evil" in the extreme case of the bureaucratically planned and executed effort to annihilate the Jews, from Eichmann's perspective as perpetrator, is what Franz Kafka revealed from the perspective of the victim who "is caught in the trap the world has turned into," in the words of M. Kundera (*Die Kunst des Romans*, [Munich, 1987], p. 35).
3. For a sophisticated theoretical explication, see N. Luhmann, *Ökologische Kommunikation* (Opladen, 1986).
4. Hannah Arendt, *Macht und Gewalt* (Munich, 1970).
5. Ironically, this was already demonstrated in detail in 1974 by W. Häfele, the dean of German nuclear research, still self-critical in those days: "Hypotheticality and the New Challenges: The Pathfinder Role of Nuclear Energy," *Minerva* 1974, no. 1: 303–322.
6. R. Wolf, "Das Recht im Schatten der Technik," *Kritische Justiz* 19 (1986): 241–262. Reprinted as "Zur Antiquiertheit des Rechts in der Risikogesellschaft," in U. Beck, *Politik in der Risikogesellschaft* (Frankfurt a.M.: Suhrkamp Verlag, 1991), pp. 378–423.
7. Initial reflections on this are in U. Beck, *Risikogesellschaft: Auf dem Weg in eine andere Modernität* (Frankfurt, 1986; *Risk Society: Towards a New Modernity* [London, 1992]).
8. Details on this point are in U. Beck, *Gegengifte: Die organisierte Unverantwortlichkeit* (Frankfurt, 1988).
9. P. Lagadec, *Das große Risiko* (Nördlingen, 1987), p. 230.
10. F. Ewald elaborates this concept in his important book, *L'Etat providence* (Paris, 1986).

6

Science and Security

Suppose Galileo's case, natural scientist against the Church, tried in 1633 before the Holy Office in Rome, were to be reopened. The Grand Inquisitor, fed on the evening news disasters, requests a retrial. His reasons: Chernobyl, genetic engineering, and all the other various advances. What would the verdict be today?

Even a decade ago, every high school senior's heart beat for the resolute Galileo, "Yet it does move!" That was the dream of the redemptive power of science. Even Brecht's Galileo, written in exile in 1938–1939, utters the bitter but true warning: "Mind you, when you pass through Germany, keep the truth hidden under your coat." Today, too, many scientists carry their "truth" under their coat—but to keep the public's apprehensions limited.

Is it finally beginning to sink in that we are living after Nagasaki, Bhopal, and Chernobyl and before the final victory of human genetics? In the struggle between science and dogma, have we switched sides, behind our own backs, as it were? Or is it science that changed sides, so that the call "Help, science!" dies away ambiguously?

Are we being freed from the secular belief in science and technology, just as people in the age of the Reformation were "released" from the secular arms of the Church? Does the appearance of dissenting atomic scientists, geneticists, physicians, engineers, and judges represent the first wave of a scientific protestantism?

Among the many accomplishments that it celebrates, science has also managed one that it keeps secret even from itself. It has ended the true/false positivism of unambiguous empirical science, the nightmare and the credo of this century. Positivism continues to exist only as a narrow-minded, monodisciplinary consciousness, but as such it is quite effective. Like the Sorcerer's Apprentice, science has succumbed to

89

the doubt it itself set free.

Anyone who poses an arbitrary question to an arbitrarily assembled group of experts, a question such as "Is formaldehyde poisonous?," will get fifteen different answers from, say, five scientists, all the answers garnished with "yes, but" or "on the one hand ... on the other hand"—if those questioned are thoughtful. If not, one will get two or three apparently unambiguous answers.

The unambiguity of scientific statements has succumbed to the insight that they are dependent on decision making, methods, and context. A different computer, a different institute, or a different sponsor will result in a different "reality." Anything else would be a miracle and not science.

Technology and science have become an economic enterprise of mega-industrial proportions, devoid of truth or enlightenment, comparable to the medieval Church, a secular power without God. Just as the Inquisitional Church was unable to prove the existence of God, the prevailing science today is unable to prove the existence of truth. Furthermore, in the breadth of its triumph it has involuntarily and indirectly proved the contrary.

So today the question is, "What does the Holy Office of Galileo's time have in common with us?" Dogma. Our dogma is the belief in progress. The place once held by God and the Church is now held by productive forces and those who develop and administer them, science and business. Their activities have all the features of religious faith: trust in the unknown, the unseen, and the intangible.

Progress is the inversion of rational action as a "rationalization process." It is a license for the unprogrammed, unratified, permanent changing of society toward the unknown. It is insinuated, for instance, that the impending commercial biotechnical rewriting of the creation of plants, animals, and people will ultimately be turned to the good after all. But even applying the lessons of other disasters and asking "how" all this is to be accomplished is considered heretical. The presupposition is that we will consent without knowing what we are consenting to.

Art has also overtaken science in its knowledge claims. In the early years of this century, Cubism broke the fiction of the object into the ambiguity of perspectives, while at the same time the pseudo-unambiguity of empiricism still prevailed in a science that was unaware of its role as knowledge producer. Similarly, the decay of the bourgeois ideals of marriage and family, as presented on stage by Ibsen, Strindberg, and others, is only now being addressed by family sociology, and with great distaste at that; now it can no longer be concealed in statistics. Science is still repressing something that has been stimulating or crippling the narrator figure in novels since Joyce, Musil, and Thomas Mann: the naiveté of the narrator is shattered by the consciousness of construction, which forces him to make the production of the story itself a theme.

The real scandal, however, probably lies in how the natural and engineering sciences react to the threats they produce: and not just since Chernobyl, though Chernobyl made the scandal tangible for a broad public. The little difference between safety and probable safety is a gap between worlds. In the atomic age, however, everyone's survival depends on it. The engineering sciences still offer only probable safety. Their statements, therefore, remain true even if two or three nuclear power plants blow up tomorrow.

"It is precisely the interplay between theory and experiment or trial and error," wrote Wolf Häfele in 1974, still self-critical at that time, "which is no longer possible for reactor technology." In their handling of the dangers of the atomic and chemical age, the natural sciences have surreptitiously stood research on its head. Implementation takes place before testing or as a kind of testing—under the Damocles' sword of horrendous investments.

It was bad enough that it took the concrete experiment of Chernobyl to refute the safety theories of physics. Much worse, however, is that the Chernobyl incident has refuted these theories, and yet they remain "true": an event that is "almost impossible" according to probabilistic theories can occur without anyone recognizing the falsity of the theories or seeking improvements.

Natural science has metamorphosed into a kind of neo-metaphysics. While people once set out to learn from experience, today they have accommodated themselves to calculations, which are evidently immune even to the shock of experiences such as Chernobyl. The earthquake of 1755 in Lisbon provoked a widespread intellectual aftershock. Today, while the untested speculations that nuclear power plants could be safe for 10,000 years are crashing down all around us, the scientists in charge tolerate talk of "Communist" reactors and return to business as usual. Mistakes that have cost billions can no longer be admitted.

Actually, Chernobyl is only the most spectacular case; let us mention another example: acceptable levels of toxins. If one applies the most elementary rules of logic to the relevant statutes and practices, the entire structure collapses. What we find are false conclusions, fallacies, and eyewash, which will probably prove as puzzling and outrageous to later generations as medieval belief in witchcraft is to us.

Then there is the big production made out of the polluter-pays principle or low-level contamination. It is the same everywhere: the norms are no longer right. The same procedure is followed everywhere: please protect the toxins from the people who are threatening them. We have known for a long while that the rules of strict causality are not applicable to globally crosslinked environmental hazards.

The leveling approach of risk calculus, which measures risks in probabilities, is a poor cure, since nuclear, chemical, and genetic megarisks have abolished the accident—at least as a spatially and temporally limited event. The consequences extend across countries and generations and can be freed from their individual anonymity only after a statistical wrestling match.

The sale of indulgences was enough to provoke Luther to nail his 95 Theses to the door of the Schlosskirche in Wittenberg; the issue, superficially, was "only" the greed of the Church. Today the issue is the survival of all of us. Where is a scientific Luther who will reproach the popes of science for their sins against the spirit of empirical science and humanity, and thus ignite the desperately needed struggle over a thorough cognitive reform of the sciences?

No one is as blind as someone who does not want to see. In his autobiography Arthur Koestler describes how he saw the suffering of the people and the symptoms of the Stalinist terror quite clearly as he traveled through the Soviet Union in 1932, but he was able to explain them away with his well-schooled cadre's mind. Have today's sciences— in training and research—become a kind of cadre school that teaches people how to fail to perceive the threatening reality they systematically produce?

But the ignorance probably has deeper and simpler causes. It is not necessary to learn from one's mistakes. Pardon me for saying it, but religion is dispensable; however, anyone who doubts whether technology and science are necessary might just as well doubt whether it will be necessary to breathe tomorrow.

The greater the threat, the greater the dependence on science. In shock from the disaster of Chernobyl, everyone suddenly talks about becquerels, rem, MCA, and glycol as if he knows what such terms mean. No doubt about it, after the next accident (and there is certain to be one), chairs will be endowed for the study of radioactive cabbage and early childhood nuclear anxiety. Refutation equals expansion; danger forces belief back onto the stage.

Unlike that of medieval Catholicism, science's Holy Office doesn't even need an Inquisition, since in scientific society the power of technology grows along with its mistakes. Even technology's harshest critics have to change their speech: that is, they have to adopt the fundamental mistakes they are opposing before they can even open their mouths.

Does that mean that a new class, a scientific-technical intelligentsia, is reaching for power? To assert that would be to once again confuse indispensability with power; but if everyone indispensable held power, then one could say that the slaves rule in a slave society. Even the medical scientists who have managed to conduct a wedding in a test tube are employees who can be fired or not promoted.

Hannah Arendt found the appropriate expression for the situation toward which we are drifting: "no-man's rule." She immediately added that this is the most tyrannical of all forms of dominance, because there is—apparently—ultimately no one who can be called to account. The other side of no-man's rule is the responsibility of the many, who, against their own better judgment, are not ready to accept the consequences of their actions.

This end of excuses certainly applies to science. No excuse is right anymore. "Unseen consequences" (yesterday's moral license) break up while being investigated, and only live on subjectively as ignorance, or reluctance to read. Research has become practice (in nuclear physics or genetic engineering) and our criticism of technology and business ought to be directed at ourselves.

What does the old term "value-free" mean now, when chemical and physical formulas can develop a political explosivity far beyond that of even the most apocalyptic language of radical social thinkers? And I would like to know by what right a science that has cast the entire world into doubt is able to declare its own foundations sacrosanct.

We must install brakes and steering gear in the "no-man's control" of a science careening out of control; we must change its self-concept and its political arrangement. The very first step must be the revival of the ability to learn and the ability to admit errors.

Human failure is not the root of all evil, as people try to convince us after each "impossible" accident. Quite to the contrary, it is an effective protection against technocratic visions of omnipotence. We human beings make mistakes. That is perhaps the only certainty we have left. We have a right to error. A development that excludes this right will push us to dogmatism or into the abyss, and perhaps both.

And for that reason, criticism on the spot in the centers of techno-industrial development gains a primary importance. Only where nuclear physics is challenged by nuclear physics, medicine by medicine, information technology by information technology, human genetics by human genetics, can the hazards for the future in the test tube become visible from outside. Critique and resistance in the technical professions serve the survival of us all.

7

Eugenics of the Future

"It's enough to make you convert to Catholicism!" exclaimed a committed feminist during a discussion of the consequences of reproductive medicine and human genetic research. Notice: in the pro and contra over the Eighth Day of commercial Creation, which dawned some time ago with the triumph of genetic technology, well-practiced antagonisms are blurring and shifting. There is a broad disquiet at large, comparable only to the "nuclear discontent"—which reaches even into the ranks of staunch believers in technology.

But the triumph of genetic technology seems to be taking place beyond society's yes or no. Even the generalizations in which its advocates seek refuge from the growing pressure for justification are difficult to break open. Certainly, the attempts to soothe the public by comparing genetic technology to things that have been familiar for centuries, such as cheese-making or beer-brewing, resemble comparing the construction of a nuclear reactor to the manufacture of pliers. But what actually is the new and alarming aspect of this technology? The successes of reproductive medicine and genetic research are making possible a kind of biopolitics: the shaping of subjectivity and society by genetic technology.

It is more than a linguistic inaccuracy to say that people want to combat congenital *diseases*. Actually, this abolishes the congenitally *diseased*, that is to say, people, people who certainly do not want their lives and experiences reduced to this single characteristic. But this touchy distinction is precisely what we must emphasize, because in the future the label "congenitally diseased" will be tantamount to a death sentence in the workshops of genetic medicine, and because this is an extreme form of reification that reduces human existence to a single pathological characteristic. Furthermore, there are worlds of difference

95

between these two concepts, worlds that separate surgery in its conventional form from the genetic surgery of the future.

The surgeon of the classical type snips away at bones, hearts, or kidneys, but always on a living, anesthetized human body; genetic surgery is concerned only with substances, test tubes, and formulas, but this abstractness has a direct impact on human subjectivity. Mastery of nature and of human beings coincide, become materially short-circuited and operable.

Genetics is a technology of the future, a technology that is shaping the expression of future life in its material substrate. Someone who can alter entire generations is no longer dealing with a person in human form but, rather, with what seems to be dead matter that can be arbitrarily and "painlessly" selected and instrumentalized according to certain features.

To give an example: a person who would combat schizophrenia genetically will, if successful, achieve something analogous to what the eugenics movements of the nineteenth and twentieth centuries proposed but were able to put into reality, if at all, only after unbelievable cruelties: the elimination of people afflicted with schizophrenia. The effect is the same, it is even incomparably intensified and more efficient; the method is different, as are, probably, most of the guiding ideas.

With the meteoric progress of prenatal diagnosis and with legalized abortion, human modes of existence are becoming technologically controllable. Anyone who speaks of "genetic diseases" is objectively promoting, in a much more elegant and effective way, the cause of eugenics.

According to the still prevailing ideology, technology is neutral. Only its use decides whether it serves "good" or "bad" ends. This self-protective assertion of science, this defensive belief in the immaculate conception of technological accomplishments, has lacked persuasive power since the atom bomb at the latest; and genetic engineering is its express refutation.

Every intervention in the genetic substance of plant, animal, and human life, interventions that are made possible by successes in genetic research, means a practical selection—that is, the elimination of some developmental variants and the promotion or improvement of other variants—on some criterion or other (such as health or productivity.) Statements about the structures of cell nuclei contain their own application and—independent of concrete purposes, contexts, and intents—they aim at selection, promotion, improvement, and recombination, that is, at fashioning or creating life, including human life.

True, Huxley's "Brave New World" is not found in any political program. Almost everyone works on, investigates, and propagates the new technologies in the firm conviction that race theories and their eugenic madness have disappeared forever in the mass graves of the Nazi terror. While the political executors of the eugenic race theories had only primitive technical means at their disposal—forced sterilization, legal prohibitions to marriage, and mass killing—which they had to apply to living people by means of malicious propaganda, social hysteria, and violent bureaucracies (from legislation to crematoria regulations), the new genetic technologies are eugenic in the logic of their actions.

For the moment, the achievements of genetic technology will not create a political eugenics that transforms a country into a gang of murderers for the persecution and annihilation of other races, beliefs, and scientific tolerators. There are no race theories, there is no eugenic movement (of the type, for instance, that exerted considerable influence in the United States earlier this century) for the very reason that the new technologies enable the *practice* of eugenics without eugenics, without any application of violence; a practice based on the possible alteration of the genetic equipment of life in all its manifestations in the test tube, clinically neutral, ideology-free, and without a bureaucracy of oppression.

Human genetics is the result of a certain concept of the human being. In the course of science, humanity has planned itself as a mechanism and now discovers its center as a formula, a mixed relationship of chemical substances and biological cells. Nothing intrinsically human has emerged or sprung forth in this case, no matter how much we might want it. Therefore it cannot be injured.

"The ova that have begun to live, to divide themselves, all look the same," says Jacque Testart, who was celebrated six years ago as the "father" of the first French test-tube baby and who today strongly criticizes this development. In the abstractness of the laboratory, while dealing with the chemical banality of substances that seem to the researcher to be just as abstract as the formulas that describe them (or perhaps fail to describe them), it is possible for the boundaries between death and life to be shifted arbitrarily far in a nominalistic and unempirical direction. Nothing feels pain, nothing responds, nothing resists Accordingly, even talking about eugenics seems to be insignificant blather from Stone Age fanatics who simply don't realize that the human essence for which they struggle exists only as a myth, a refuted working hypothesis.

Life? It's just a celebratory platitude, a necessary invention of public relations to allow the pursuit of research work that will go on anyway with less distraction behind the screens put up to block out responsibility. It is precisely the fact that the researcher doesn't see or feel or hear a living thing that predestines the biotechnical unity of research and practice to act as selection labs that have nothing in common with concentration camps, but whose effects are functionally comparable. One can no longer know what the effects will be, and thus anything can become routine. Forgetting and repression are no longer necessary, since knowledge was never present.

The eugenics of the future does not act directly on the soul by means of law or poison gas. That horrible early form of eugenics, which was applied to the whole society, has been historically discarded. In the abstract "test-tube eugenics" of the future, preventive-technical means will replace discrimination and killing. Its representatives need not know, believe, or say anything about race theories, since technology itself accomplishes the "improvement" in a realm beyond social and ideological hysteria.

We are dealing, then, not with a political or social eugenics but, rather, with a "merely" technological eugenics, which, however, remains silent about its goals by virtue of the force and neutrality of its realization. That is precisely why it is today able to progress unopposed, on the scale of and according to the principles of industrial mass production, in the guise of being a precaution and with the scientific blessings of genetic counseling.

Barbarism can occur because it does not present itself in the familiar garb of political brutality. It approaches in the clinic, the laboratories, and the plants of the new biotechnical industries. It does not start with riots in the streets, the persecution of minorities, mass rallies, or the abolition of parliament. This time it takes the stage in white lab coats, equipped with research ambitions; in the good intentions of physicians; and in parents' desire to do the "best" for their children. The courts and parliament concur, because when the flag of health is waved, people always applaud enthusiastically.

Who wants to hamper the genetic control of congenital diseases and thereby become an advocate of continuing disease? What is so bad about parents' wanting "healthy" babies? Where is the horror in the efforts for "more productive" types of plants and animals?

The eugenics that threatens us has taken off the trappings of a sinister conspiracy and put on the costume of health, productivity, and promises of profit. It receives its momentum from the dramaturgy of the threats to which it must respond (AIDS, ecological destruction) and from the enforcement power of billion-dollar investments. It enters the stage of world history as "commercial eugenics."[1]

Certainly our society is dominated by free will—at least here and for the time being. (We shall leave aside for a moment what the triumph of genetic technology threatens in countries and cultures with different political systems, values, and ideology.) But "free will" has the old scornful sound. It has the concealed connotation of a lost social consciousness, as if there were no institutions or interests that could use free will to establish themselves; as if free will were an escape from the distress of parents who either have to justify a "genetic defect," a "handicap," in their children to those children themselves (as they earlier had to demand of God in silent prayers), or who have to become the executors of a eugenics that often enough discriminates against them as well for carrying the same "defect." The helpless parents meet again in the nightmare of a technically developed, quasi-divine creator role, which is an irresponsible responsibility in either case.

The development of the ability to genetically create or restore means, for the parents, that the socially determined ideas of an "ideal child" can be more effectively established even in the pre-embryonic stage. If things continue in this direction the role heretofore played by types of baby food, nursing periods, and parents' help with school work may in the future be played by genetic screening and counseling and the operational selection of "career genes" to decide a child's future in the competition of society: genetic technology instead of education.[2]

Embryonic or pre-embryonic "quality control" can be observed today in the selection of candidates for semen donation and surrogate motherhood. "A physician in Essen," writes Elisabeth Beck-Gernsheim, "with a practice specializing in artificial insemination, cites the following categories, among others, for selecting semen donors: 'no protruding ears or hook noses, at least 5 foot 8 inches tall, no flipped-out types, people from settled circumstances.' Such procedures are . . . certainly not meant as a type of eugenics or selective breeding. . . . But what does 'unacceptable' mean to a 'client'—a black semen donor for whites perhaps? What is a 'defect'—protruding ears for instance?"[3]

It is possible that ideas about who is "fit to live" or "unfit to live," still slumbering in the collective unconsciousness, may be reawakened by the scent of technological possibilities. Under the seemingly neutral label of "biogenetic defects," people's prejudices can now use the Final Solution of genetic surgery, not to eliminate the victim of their unmastered fears—that would be putting it too harshly—but, rather, to prevent it from even coming into being on the way to perfecting the human race.

This danger of a medically implicit eugenics is growing with the scope of medical diagnostics and surgery, along with the gray zones and social prejudices embedded in them. With irritating insensitivity, in an official information publication, the [German] Federal Ministry of Justice already recommends "preventing the danger of transmission of severe congenital diseases by taking the family history of the semen donor."

The promise of health makes "free will" slippery, and makes it almost impossible to decide against genetic technology, which can be virtually assured of success because of the costs that society incurs from the "luxury" of congenital diseases. The inquiry into health becomes a pre-natal death sentence that will silently, softly, and clinically straighten the "crooked sticks," as the elder Kant called us human beings.

Notes

1. Jeremy Rifkin, *Kritik der reinen Unvernunft* (Reinbek, 1987).
2. Elisabeth Beck-Gernsheim, *Technik, Macht und Moral—Über Fortpflanzungstechnologie und Gentechnologie* (Frankfurt, 1991). English translation, *Technology, the Market, and Morality* (Atlantic Highlands, N.J., 1995).
3. Ibid.

8

The World as Laboratory

Any contemplation of the interlocking of progress and destruction or the growth of hazards and the economy must struggle with a word that sticks to these efforts like a bad smell: "repetition." Everything has been said, exchanged, balanced, repeated. For some time we have been stuck in the repetition of repetition, and any contribution that gets readers' attention can claim to be original only if there are big gaps in what people have read—but such a claim can count on success particularly because of scientific specialization and detail work. What would have been left out anyway? What thought is not already turning brown somewhere in the dusty corners of libraries?

Science and the technology spree, with which the industrial age feeds and irresistibly drives its transformation of the world into world markets, take place as a kind of undemocratic, permanent change in all areas of life, and may even openly contradict the schoolbook rules of democracy. We know this and have thoroughly discussed it, but that has not really kept us from accepting the contradiction. Consider as an example the tinkering advances in knowledge in genetic technology and human genetics and their impending large-scale utilization: there is no site and no subject for decision making in this area of progress, an area that will touch, change, and quite possibly endanger the human substance of our social life.

New technology weasels its way in, advancing here and there, as support for points of view that are motivated by completely different priorities (curiosity, career, competition, opening markets, protecting investments). Making such an amorphous process the business of parliament is as absurd as an Eskimo's wish to take a summer vacation to Greenland. One can criticize science and technology again and again, in philosophical journals, in articles for the art-and-living sections of newspapers,

101

and again in trade-union monthlies. There are honors and academies for doing so; perhaps there will someday be almost professionally protected Cassandra careers, with opportunities for streets to be named posthumously in one's honor. But who really cares about that?

Overpowering objections await anyone who questions the status quo: Should seeking the truth perhaps be replaced by voting? And all this talk of an *alternative* science! Is logic flexible? Can it be laid out broadly or narrowly, violently or gently?

Such prickly arguments lie in wait everywhere to burst the soap-bubble dreams of an alternative development of technology and industry. Does the call for control and shared decision making not throttle freedom of research? Isn't it therefore in the same unsavory group as the Inquisition, fascism, and Stalinism, which also subjugated the freedom of scientific judgment, albeit in different ways? To complete the triumph over the critic of science, already down for the count: what will be the source of the social force and power, the rationality, that are needed to break the spell over the Sorcerer's Apprentice? Doesn't all the puzzling over possibilities for political direction and co-decision seem ridiculous in view of a global, autonomous mechanism of progress? Doesn't shaking up the somnambulistic certainty of techno-scientific civilization just rouse the spirits of irrationalism? How in the world is the ecological catastrophe to be mastered, if not by an upward turn in technological development? But that means *more*, rather than less, technological rule is required, so that any critique of progress, if it is fortunate enough to succeed, only raises the technological programming and planning of society to a higher level. Isn't the call for alternatives just a cheap way to create new world markets? Isn't the dramatization of ecological threats already introducing a new technological imperialism of the First World over the Third and Fourth Worlds? This is how the questions march over the critics of progress.

Here I introduce and test a question so obviously banal that it might again be worth wasting one's attention on it.

PROGRESS ALSO MEANS: FROM THE SCIENCE OF TRUTH TO SCIENCE AS IF AND BUT

The power that can counter the autonomous development of science and technology does not, in the first instance, consist of politics, parliament, law, the public sphere, or meetings of citizens' initiative groups. All these countervailing institutions can only gain influence to the extent that they recognize and politically use science itself to undermine the autonomous course of science and technology. Science and technology, with their inherent thoroughness, reveal possible starting points for their own reformation. The still unseen side effect of the techno-scientific revolution is the revolutionizing of the sciences themselves, the overthrow of their foundations and the claims with which they started and established their autonomous course.

To restate it bluntly, all attempts to attribute a logic to the progress of the sciences, to base their judgment-making ability on the infallibility of experiments, to represent the sciences as, in a way, nature's finding a voice, all these have failed. It was always—and this is important—the advances in science itself that demolished the designs of scientific rationality. Modern physics destroyed the old mechanistic causal understanding of nature and human beings. Epistemology and the theory of science have cut off any path leading to reality in and of itself, without the surmising and erring recourse to knowledge. Progress in science, after all, means the continual refutation of older conceptions, and thus it is a constant testimony within our memory, reaching beyond the present moment, to human and scientific inadequacy.

The self-abdication of science is not, therefore, bad science, some sort of flaw or mistake that could be removed. It is the product of the law of "further, more, better" that is an intrinsic part of science, and only through a temporary forgetting occasioned by the elation of current knowledge can it be distorted into infinite progress. We are largely concerned with a development of science and technology that charges forward without benefit of truth or methodological certainty in its statements and projects. This is a science, then, that has metamorphosed by virtue of its own judgment, its own mechanism of progress, from a science of truth into a science of it and but.

In a certain way, the ancient Greek Skeptics' surmise that our ignorance grows with our knowledge is being confirmed today. The result of scientific progress is not security but uncertainty, although a considered, questioned, and more conscious uncertainty. We know less because we know more. Ignorance and the awareness of ignorance grow along with knowledge, and this publicly reflected doubt, which is the quintessence of science on the leading edge of research, is the core of the uneasiness that shakes techno-scientific civilization today. Cultural critique and the critique of science would have remained unsuccessful, as in the past, if science had not entered a stage of published and objectified self-doubt as a consequence of its specialized autonomy. The doubt that resides in the deepest recess of scientific rationality, constitutes it, and is (involuntarily) unleashed in its most advanced stage is the inside ally, the door-opener, for a future reformation of science in a society that is becoming mature with and against science.

SOCIETY AS LABORATORY: DEMOCRACY SNEAKS IN

These considerations sound very philosophical, which nowadays means remote. The opposite is true: these are stumbling blocks in laboratory and research practice.

Schoolbooks distinguish between pure science and applied science. The former is research and the latter is technology. The former is free (value-free) and the latter is determined by and interlocked with economics and politics. Rationality protects pure research under the honorary title of "basic research"; the term claims first, a sequential, and second, a derivational, relationship between research and application, between experiment and technical utilization. This entire ideal world of scientific rationality has collapsed, like a house of cards, under the weight of the largest, deepest, and most economically ambitious advances of recent years. Theories on the operation and safety of nuclear power plants, for instance, can only be tested *after* construction. Experimental mega-technology must be stage-managed and monitored after implementation *as* the manufacture of a new, unknown, and unexplored reality.

Practice as research and running risks for their own sake are two sides of the same thing in the adventure of technological civilization.

We now know that many, at least two hundred, experiments of "destructive embryonic research" where needed to achieve the first test-tube baby. Nuclear reactors must be *built*, artificial biotechnical creatures must be *released into* the environment, and chemical products must be *put into circulation* for their properties, safety, and long-term effects to be studied. Moral, political, and logical problems lurk in this reversal of experiment and application, in this fusion of research and technology into a new type of *manufacturing tinker-science*, in a society that is itself becoming experimental. So far, only the ethical problems have been (cautiously) revealed in public. They are as evident in embryonic research as in open-air experiments, and they lead to difficult trade-offs and conflicts whose insolubility creates a virtually predictable obscurity that is considered worthy of encouragement, for it then allows one to write off ethical problems as lost causes. In this sense, the establishment of ethics chairs at universities is the second another way of preserving a green light for research.

The dilemma lies in the fact that the experiment is exported and *society is made into a laboratory*, which has two consequences.[1]

First, research becomes a kind of groping in the fog. Laboratory experiments assume that variables are controllable. To the extent the boundaries of the laboratory are opened this controllability is cancelled.

Experiments in the open air and on people (as represented not only by genetic engineering, research into human genetics, and reproductive medicine, but also by ecological catastrophes) raise not only ethical problems but also theoretical questions about the logic of research. When the controllability of the laboratory situation is lost, so is the very framework that makes a precise conceptualization and determination of variables possible at all. Checking hypotheses becomes blurred, fictive, because the opening of the laboratory boundaries requires one to assume theoretically and practically uncontrollable influences.

Second, manufacturing as technology research becomes politically dependent on consent and responses to public questions and doubts, which scientific authority and scientific logic cannot answer or defuse. Active science needs deeds, manufactured realities, to correct its mistakes. It becomes a layperson in its own case, however, when what is at stake is deciding whether it is acceptable to risk the adventure of a science that is first an initially practical and only second empirical and theoretical, science and that at the same time cancels the cultural constants of life. The precondition for manufacturing as research is a consensus that cannot be based on science, but only on politics.

The risk of a technology research that studies created facts can never be logically and morally legitimized in a scientific sense. Genetic engineers, human geneticists, reactor researchers, practitioners of reproductive medicine and the like become beggars or solicitors for their own cause. Their activity becomes dependent on public and political consent, without a hint of scientific justification. Politics comes before research, and research really and literally becomes politics itself, because it must produce and change something in order to develop its scientific rationality at all.

Where science robs itself of its own scientific character, however, it opens the door to public disputes, fears, and viewpoints and to shared decisions. Democracy sneaks in, not only in the implementation but also in the uncertainty and conflict over the direction of research itself, before that research can develop and stage-manage its own objective course of events. In starting research, the scientist is a layperson, ignorant like other observers and affected people. No, more than that: he is a layperson *with interests*. His research interests *compel* him to prove that the experiment is harmless. Bias is a professional necessity, because questions and doubts, now ruthless and fundamental, can literally starve technological research. To put it metaphorically, the suspected thief passes judgment on a robbery.

We have arrived at the central problem. We can learn from our mistakes; according to Popper, this is the core of scientific rationality. Who will decide, however—how, when and upon what basis—whether a social experiment of production as technological research has failed? Research that must become practice in order to be research has leveraged away its conditions of falsification. The boundaries between production, research, and use are blurring. Furthermore, all accidents and disruptions—for instance, in nuclear power plants all over the world—are experimental findings in a continuing, perhaps undecidable concrete experiment.

But many voices are involved in this experiment. Differing, antagonistic worldviews appear. The technical people are interested in technical success, which may well be independent of health effects, social and political turbulence and responsibilities, and lest we forget, the verdict of profitability. A chorus of voices and viewpoints argues about the course and outcome of such experiments.

Two things stand out here. The experiment, nuclear energy for instance, becomes *inconcludable, temporally, spatially and socially.* At the same time, however, there is no experimenter in charge, *no decision maker* to decide on the validity of the initial hypothesis with scientific authority. In the limiting case, we are concerned with all-inclusive experiments on humanity itself (therefore not experiments at all), whose unwritten, controversial history, across time, disciplines, and nations, corresponds to the results of earlier experiments.

If we apply Popper's rather antiquarian sounding dictum to this situation, which has existed for some time and is by now well established, then scientific rationality hangs on the silk thread of the revisability and the fallibility of research that creates its own reality. Nuclear power plants could still be shut down and removed from the power grid, although with great difficulty and at high costs. What will happen, however, to the flesh-and-blood "mistakes" of the genetic engineers and human geneticists? How can research be kept capable of learning when to admit mistakes not only destroys billion-dollar investments but is tantamount to the self-annihilation of an entire specialized discipline? The new research installations know the laboratory only as a way station; they need practice, open-air experiments, and social change to test their assumptions. Hence they are struggling in a totally new way with dogma, not in terms of their objective intentions but in view of the displaced, inverted, interest constellations of their production as research. There is justified suspicion that the ability to make mistakes and learn is fundamentally truncated. Science has said goodbye to its logic and now comes under the power of dogmas that it itself created and cultivated. Furthermore, this is occurring in those scientific fields and research issues that touch and change the very form of existence of life and humankind.

THE RISK CALCULUS; OR, HOW DO WE WANT TO LIVE?

We know how these issues are treated *de facto*, People form special installations for risk calculations, which are attempts to produce, by technical means, answers to the very questions that elude purely technical answers. The currently ubiquitous talk of risks is a mathematically concealed form of moralizing. Accepted risks are compared with risks that one proposes to accept, whereby the legitimation that the former enjoy is supposed to be transferred to the latter.

It is undeniable that the calculus of risks strips some of the excitement from the adventure of industrialism. Unpredictable future events become calculable in the present. Their effects are elevated above the suffering of the individuals involved and become events predicted probabilistically, and therefore parts of the system that require general regulation, through insurance policies, for instance, or technical precautions, burden sharing, preventive medical care, and so on. This does not change the fact that technology cannot, by inherent, mathematical means, on its own responsibility, as it were, solve the political and ethical questions that assail it.

On the contrary, risk calculations are a kind of bankruptcy declaration of technical rationality. They never lead to what they were supposed to produce, namely, acceptance. Specialists depend on cultural and ethical standards to investigate the limits of what is tolerable and acceptable. "Maximum allowable levels" are traffic rules, basic laws for dealing with predictably unpredictable effects of techno-industrial developments. Special knowledge of reactions, processes, and medical effects contribute to them, but answers to the question "How should we live?" also contribute. Not only can that question be answered differently from one country to another, from one culture to another, but further, in a democratically governed society, it does not belong just in the hands of engineers. Nevertheless, technology and engineers have a monopoly on questions of risk in Germany as in other industrialized countries. Even reservations about the risks of a technology are almost always formulated on the basis of techno-scientific thinking. The therapies and alternatives offered also originate in the arsenal of technology.

There are demands for scrubbing technologies to eliminate emissions containing sulfur dioxide, and catalytic converters are supposed to prevent harmful automobile exhaust gases. From recycling plans to containment devices for nuclear power plants, the call for legislation usually demands nothing more than changing the signals in environmental policy in favor of an allegedly better *technical* solution. Many petitions presented in court demand nothing more, as the complainants understand it, than making the insights of natural science legally binding. Acceptable levels for pollution are cast into doubt because the scientific knowledge on which they rest seems to be outdated or the measuring procedures are technologically obsolete. The emissions of older facilities are subject to criticism whenever the people affected suspect that they exceed what is "inevitable" according to the state of the art.

The engineers have hung their society-creating role on a simple-minded social nail. They are conceded the right, obligatory for law and politics, to decide, on their own standards, what the state of the art requires. But since this general restriction is the standard for legally required safety, private organizations and committees (for example in Germany, the Society of German Engineers or the German Standards Institute) decide *de facto* what amount of threat all of us should accept.

In air pollution policy, noise protection, water policy, and so on, one finds the same pattern over and over again. Laws specify the general political plan, but only the fine print reveals what ration of standardized pollution the citizens are subject to. Even the classical instruments of political control—statutes and administrative regulations—are hollow, juggling with the state of the art and thereby undermining their own jurisdiction. At the same time they install "techno-scientific expert knowledge" on the throne of risk civilization.

WHAT IS TO BE DONE?
PERSPECTIVES OF AN
ECOLOGICAL ENLIGHTENMENT

All the arguments that I have highlighted here can be turned around and read the other way. In its most advanced stage, science has become an undertaking of involuntary self-subversion not in narrow-minded specialization but in the interrelationship between disciplines, times, theories, schools, and methods. It is scientific meticulousness that honeycombs the armor protecting the scientific monopoly on knowledge. In the same measure, external agencies gain opportunities to influence not just the evaluation but also the design of scientific knowledge. This must be used for a democratic opening and shared decision making.

Society itself has become a laboratory; that is, finding the truth has become both polyvocal and public. There are specialists for the technical matters and the effects; social and functional realities split apart and compete. The "simple" (i.e., traditional and monopolistic) concept of science and a "reflexive" (i.e., self-critical) one begin to orient and organize themselves *inside* the disciplines. In matters of risk, and this is important, no one is an expert. If the engineers have the say here *de facto*, then it is important to open the committees and the circles of experts and evaluators to the pluralism of disciplines, extradisciplinary modes of judgment, and shared decision making that have already been speaking out for some time and have begun to organize themselves.

The principle of the separation of powers needs to be enforced against the technocratic unity of culprits and judges (expert witnesses). Precisely because the investigation of effects and risks presumes their production, others—laypeople, the public sphere, the parliament, and politics—must also have a say; they must regain the power to make decisions in a society that has gone over to shaping its future through technology. The investigation of threats and risks is a necessary first step from the isolation of scientific social change into the public sphere.

Scientific activity requires justification on the basis of standards, which are concealed in the Trojan Horse of shared decision making. And yet it must be seen just as clearly that risk is a concept of only limited use for restraining or steering an autonomous, dynamic technologizing of society.

Risks can be minimized technically. Anyone who depends on them as the only lever to gain and expand some public say in the techno-scientific adventure puts pressure on himself to consent when the safety concerns are alleviated. Democracy beyond expertocracy—and expertocracy is a particular danger when hazards are dramatized—begins where debate and decision making are opened about whether we *want* a life under the conditions that are being presented to us even by those technologies that are growing steadily safer.

How do we want to live? The concentration on risks and safety can wrest this question away from public responsibility, which alone is qualified to answer it in a democracy that does not wish to capitulate to the shaping power of technology. A key question for present and future social development is, Can—or, more optimistically, how can—the industrial system learn from its mistakes? That the industrial system can *profit* from its mistakes is proved by the expanding market for anything labeled "environmentally safe" (from shoelaces to motor oil). Recruiting industrial production's interest in technology and using economic recovery to solve questions of survival is an obvious step toward a successful pragmatic policy, in the best sense of the word, of preventing and overcoming hazards. The industrial system and its productivity, set on an ecological path, point the way out of the dilemma of an industrial production trapped between growth and destruction. The magic formula is this: we need not just a social but also an *ecological* market economy.

In his most recent book, *Der Ökologische Umbau der Industriegesellschaft* (*The Ecological Reconstruction of Industrial Society*, 1989), Joschka Fischer (who represents many in the Social Democratic Party and the Christian Democratic Union as well as his fellow Greens), clearly and with laudable specificity sketched this one logically possible way. One can feel a lot of sympathy for his pragmatism, precisely because it is so nicely un-German and dismisses purism as ridiculous in favor of an orientation toward practical effect, which means the detailed treatment of hazards. This realism is also what may finally make the Greens electable.

None of this, however, must prevent us from seeing pragmatism as the fundamental mistake, which stands out when one considers the question, "To what hazard targets should the ecological reconstruction of industrial society be oriented?" To those that may or may not be brought into the open, into public view in ten years, or today, or tomorrow? The recent history of mega-hazards is enough to make one suspicious here. How long was nuclear energy generally welcomed? When were the ozone hole and forest destruction estimated, or statistically discounted, and what were the counter-arguments, the loaded counter-questions?

It becomes clear that a pragmatic approach to techno-economic hazards is taken in by ad-hoc definitions, forgets its own historical origin and uses the highly changeable media image of recognized hazards, or those struggling for recognition, as the plumb-line of a substantive social reconstruction. The category error lies in the technological verification of hazards and, the concomitant exclusion of their social genesis of hazards and their conditions.

Only by breaking if the law of unseen side effects, by elevating decision making on technologies to public and political processes before and during the genesis of hazards, can we return the fate of the hazard civilization to the realm of action and decision-making. We must reverse the prevailing practice of developing and financing new technologies first, and then investigating the effects and the hazards, and finally publicly discussing them under the guillotine of manufactured objective constraints. Only in that way could we minimize the hazards *and* open the possibilities for people to have a say in the matter. This time (for once) the political and democratic opening of hazard technocracy is also a way to prevent the hazards.

Note

1. See also Joschka Fischer, "Die Krise der Umweltpolitik," in Beck, *Politik in der Risikogesellschaft* (Frankfurt a.M.: Suhrkamp, 1991), pp. 312–329.

9

Blind Realism: Sociology and the Crises of Industrial Modernity

That society is subject to historical changes is among the few generalizations that sociologists can agree on. But anyone who knows sociological debates from the inside knows that this generalization is applied almost exclusively to premodern societies. Developed industrial states, according to their own understanding and that of sociology, are supposed to have reached the culmination of social history, their future will be only more and better of the same. To be sure, one does hear talk of *post* industrialism or *late* capitalism, but that should not mislead us into believing that anything more than mere modification of the developmental dynamic of modern industrial society is being considered. The diagnosis runs: transformation, restrained and unrestrainable— but without transformation. One industrial revolution engulfs the next. After each, however, what comes into being is in essence industrial society. That is what the theoretical constructs of sociology still amount to.

Even in 1968, at the peak of student unrest, the turbulent sociologists' convention in Frankfurt was dominated—one almost has to say united—by the controversy over "late capitalism or industrial society?" No one doubted the efficacy and the inherent dynamism of industrial modernity, that is the primacy of business and industry, the triumph of technology and science, and the concomitant "de-mystification" of social action. The Frankfurt School, having dismissed the proletariat much earlier, and the search for other exponents of enlightenment having been fruitless, people even agreed that capitalist industrial development had cushioned itself against its inherent crises through the development of social wealth.

The West German welfare-state boom and the disciplining of class antagonisms that it made possible led a historically sensitive theorist like Jürgen Habermas to question the potential of Marxist class and crisis theory to address crises. The multiplication of the concept of crisis that he subsequently suggested in the early 1970s, however, points to the bankruptcy of the attempt to use Marx to save Marx: one has to deal with the historical experience of capitalist stability through two world wars, contrasting constitutions, fascism, and economic crises. This requires sacrifices and differentiations that not only take the sting out of the concept of crisis by multiplying it, but also render it theoretically ineffective: many crises but no crisis.

Why all the fuss then? Why the stigmatization of The Frankfurt School? It was ultimately more a matter of contrasting evaluations, in a deeper sense the practice and foundation of publicly effective social criticism in post-war Germany with its imposed democracy, and less a disagreement over the diagnosis of society. Even in the *Dialectic of Enlightenment*, Horkheimer and Adorno essentially agree with their positivistic opponents that technocracy is powerful and irresistible.[1] Given their commitment to the original hopes of the Enlightenment, it is precisely this assessment that underlies their pessimistic vision of social development.

The idea that enlightenment, turned technical, can end up in barbarism is not at all farfetched, especially today. Every intervention in the genetic substance of plant, animal, and human life made possible by the research successes of reproductive medicine and molecular biology in practice implies a selection,—that is, the elimination of some developmental variants of life, for whatever motive (health, achievement), and the promotion or improvement of others.

Such themes are seldom investigated in sociology. Sociology is a community of dissidents from sociology. The great controversies have fallen silent, and not without reason. In the past sociology has expanded theoretically, has become socially acceptable, and has been laboriously covered over by conflicting theoretical languages and methodological conceptions—and it has skidded into an unproductive consensus that now prevents it from even perceiving the great social upheavals and challenges, much less considering them creatively in an effort encompassing the entire discipline. Banished to the sidelines of the great social debates over the techno-ecological challenges of industrial society, many sociologists cannot suppress the vague feeling that sociology as a science of reality no longer understands social reality, for all the brilliance of its empiricism.

Even the conceptions of the "postindustrial society" that Daniel Bell and Alain Touraine outlined in the late 1960s work with only one variation of social reality: the shift in the center of gravity from the production to the service sector.[2] Great hopes were tied to that. However, the research that Touraine's and Bell's work stimulated shows first, that liberation from the burden of industrial labor relies on a false clarity of the concept of service and, second, that the apolitical hopes err in expecting to resolve mass unemployment in industrial countries by an expansion of "services."

In the early 1970s, people began to debate the concept of the "labor society." The task was to theoretically reappraise the concept of labor, which had been pluralized by women's studies, by the counterculture movements, and by flexible working hours and employment. The increase in leisure time and more individualized work circumstances sap work of its structuring power. In the 1960s, Helmut Schelsky had already emphasized that one's profession was one of the last sources of stability, and that—together with the family—it provided inner stability in an unsettling modernity. With mass unemployment and permanent mobility, this no longer applies (if indeed it ever did apply), but this fact has not yet stimulated a search for new theories.

In recent years Michel Foucault's "disciplinary society" has been discovered. His subtle and gloomy analyses of the inescapable penetration of power into all social institutions, specifically including those that promise liberation, moved him surprisingly close to the *Dialectic of Enlightenment.* And did not Max Weber, especially in his late works, also say similar things? (This again attests that Weber not only founded sociology but will outlive it.) Reflection has "withered away" or "intensified"—as the case may be—into reflection on the classics. And why not?

Many feel that Nikals Luhmann is an exception to this; he chose to test his systems theory against the obstacle of the "ecological question." But let us hear his summation: "Our society must live with potential catastrophes on the horizon, and do so quite normally and unexcitedly; otherwise the potential catastrophes will not disappear, and will be joined by inevitable damage due to confusion."[3] Is that not, classically, the great postindustrialist late-capitalist consensus, but now bluntly cynical, without Old World lamentation? Does not sociological enlightenment therefore, end in a (theoretically obfuscated) industrial fatalism?

Thus the question: What if the *realism* of sociology has led to a consensus of Weber, Marx, Adorno, and Luhmann? Yet, it is precisely empirical research that is groaning under the burden of pressing the reality of the data into old categories. The data are already battering old concepts; alternative realities are appearing everywhere. The social sciences are being run over by developments that, according to their own categories and concepts, really ought not to exist.

Where has it been decreed that the public criticism of science and technology can no longer be placed in the old drawer of cultural criticism, simply because it uses scientific diagnoses and is proven right time after time? The consequences affect all sciences. The uniform scientific ideal has shifted surreptitiously toward the social sciences. When the natural sciences are dealing with mega-risks, they are dependent on value judgments ("acceptable levels"), and so they have become disguised "cultural sciences."

The comparative forms of the scientific method now run: truth, doubt, self-limitation. Living with unresolved conflicts even in science is something one can learn from the social sciences.

What does the social researcher do when it is no longer clear how far fundamental concepts such as occupation, family, social class, or social stratum still fit reality; when it is no longer clear whether unemployment is a social problem or the first step toward freedom from labor society? Is the striving for full employment and economic growth the solution or a cause of the problem? Are the possibilities of falling ill narrowed or broadened by an expansion of the medical-care system? The suspicion that one is driving out the Devil with Beelzebub has nestled into all areas and issues of the modernization process. The whole world of classical industrial society is in flux, and not because of "culture-critical agitation" but as a continuation of the dynamism of techno-industrialization and modernization, that was set in motion in the nineteenth century. Industrialism itself is becoming a tradition, undermining its own historically generated and historically transitory premises and life forms. Implementation turns into dissolution. This— not postindustrialism and certainly not postmodernity—is what we fail to understand theoretically and empirically. In the triumph of industrial modernity, a different social form is coming into being.

The founding fathers of sociology attempted to put it on the most stable conceptual foundations possible. The Kantian question regarding the conditions of possibility, transferred to social action and society or to capitalism and modernity, forms the common program of Marx, Weber, Durkheim, Simmel, Mead, and Parsons. The historical experiences of early industrial modernity have been made the baseline, and the search to discover what is conceptually necessary as a reaction to the collapse of the feudal metaphysical worldview has, to this day, put empirical research—including all its ramifications into family, sex roles, class, and strata—on the clay feet of transitory a prioris.

The insecurities and indistinctness of sociological statements are the insecurities and indistinctness of society as a historical "object." "At some time or other," Weber wrote, perceptively but this time against himself, "the colors change. The meaning of the unintentionally utilized points of view is becoming uncertain, the way is being lost in the dusk. The light of the great cultural problems has travelled on. Science also prepares itself to change its point of view and its conceptual apparatus."[4] He left it to us to figure out how that is done, but finding it out would be worth the effort that sociology costs us.

Notes

1. Max Horkheimer and Theodor Adorno, *Dialektik der Aufklärung* (Frankfurt, 1969).
2. Daniel Bell, *The Coming of Post-Industrial Society: A Venture in Social Forecasting* (New York: Basic Books, 1973); Alain Touraine, *La Société Post-Industrielle: Naissance d'une société* (Paris: Editions Denoel, 1969).
3. Niklas Luhmann, "Die Welt als Wille ohne Vorstellung: Sicherheit und Risiko aus der Sicht der Sozialwissenschaften," *Die politische Mainung* 229 (1986): 21.
4. Max Weber, "Die Objektivität sozialwissenschaftlicher und sozialpolitischer Erkenntnis," in *Gesammelte Aufsatze zur Wissenschafslehre* (Tubingen, 1968), 214.

10

Sociology and the
Ecological Issue

In 1984 James F. Short, president of the American Sociological Association, made a plea for opening sociology to ecological issues. He said that a sociology that was reluctant to engage in research on the ecological challenge would have to expect "that we will increasingly be seen as irrelevant to an area of extreme importance to all of humankind—an area in which the major institutions, all socities, and all nations are daily affected by analyses and decisions which remain largely uninformed by sociological theory and analyses."[1] So much for James F. Short in his inaugural address to the convention of the American Sociological Association in 1984. Now, one has to ask, so what? A sociology that worried about the ecological issue would be particularly deserving of support because it would protect society from the consequences of its activities. No matter how skeptical I may be, I cannot cast off the peculiar naiveté of believing that sociology should have something to do with understanding the society in which it acts. Let me therefore recall a few facts documenting the importance of the ecological issue for the understanding of society.

First, throughout the 1980s, ecology has been rated as being of the highest importance in German public opinion surveys. Surprisingly, that also applies, so far as I know, to former East Germany. The Germans want a Green republic, or, perhaps one should add, a Green mega-Switzerland. Being good, being Green is a documentable daydream of modern Germans. In Germany, at least, but in other European countries as well, not addressing the ecological issue means ignoring important developmental tendencies.

117

Second, in view of ecological destruction, considerable "regulatory deficits" are appearing or, in other words, institutions are encountering "grave adaptation problems." I shall select only one example from many. The regulations on maximum acceptable levels for chemical substances are oriented toward individual substances and exclude synergistic effects, even though the latter are certainly ascertainable with current methodologies. As a result, even if everyone adheres to the regulations, species die, the seas become polluted, and so on.

Third, sociology can contribute its experience in dealing with "social issues" to the scientific and political debate on "ecological issues." I am not saying that a structural analogy exists here, but it is conspicuous that much of the debate is repetition, and that both debates require a similar learning process. In any case, what is required is different institutions and not just a different ethics or a different technology.

I

If this is the case, why are there still mutual reservations and taboos against exchanges? I would like to mention and explain two points, first "background assumptions" (to borrow a phrase from Alvin Gouldner), and second, switch-settings in sociological theory. Subsequently I would like to show how sociology is beginning to open itself to the ecological issue, and where I see opportunities for access. But before that, I would like to list a few of the factors that hamper the perception of the ecological issue in sociology:

1. Along with the ecological issue and the critique of the industrial system, judgments and irrationalities rise that sociologists (among many others!) have relegated to the critique of civilization, and which they have repudiated since World War II, for good reason. Two aspects of the ecological issue arouse deep-seated reservations here. First, the critique of civilization relies on unsubstantiated and unsubstantiable value judgments and pessimism. Accordingly, the ecological critique looks like neo-Spenglerism, especially to foreign observers, reminding them of the "decliners of the West" (*Untergangster des Abendlandes*), as Karl Kraus christened this group. Second, the empirical assessments on which the critique of civilization rests have largely proved false. The examples are legion: fear of technology, Luddism, the threat of "railroad disease" (the human organism was allegedly unable to withstand a speed of 22 miles per hour) and so on. Viewed in this way, many see recognition of the ecological issue as a tardy victory of Luddites and preindustrial nature romantics.

2. Ecological definitions are mediated by the natural sciences and

are often controversial and contentious within the natural sciences. This implies that sociologists must relativize or abandon their hard-won professional autonomy and construct their analysis on the foundations of scientific results that elude their own sociological judgment.

3. The professional standing of sociology rests on refined methods and a highly developed specialist status. By contrast, the ecological issue seems oversized, disregarding national or professional boundaries. At first glance it appears that one must abandon one's well-practiced scientific standards if one is to devote oneself to the ecological issue.

4. For that reason as much as any, the ecological issue appears to many to be a scientifically dubious media spectacle, just a faddist topic: Nowhere are we dealing with a substantial "phenomenon in itself." Everything takes place inside peoples' heads, everything is interpretation and received wisdom. In contrast to serious scientific researchers, aren't journalists biased in picking out alarming news of disasters— and causes to match—and aren't they therefore setting the wrong political accents? The whole thing is probably just a contemporary phenomenon, a specter that may well disappear around the next corner of social development.

5. This seems to be corroborated by the way in which the urgency, perhaps even the reliability, of the ecological issue varies with cultural and national differences. What kind of truth is it, to adapt a phrase from Montaigne, that ends at the French border and is mere imagination or deception to the people beyond?

Taken together, these factors reinforce the skepticism of many sociologists, and of social scientists generally, regarding the ecological issue. Their reservations are by no means new or coincidental; they are connected with the very origins of sociology itself.

Sociology did not arise, nor was it conceived, as a science of the "social" or of "society," but rather as a science of *bourgeois, industrial* society, with all the controversies and varied ways of thinking contained therein. Its issues and polarities reflect the issues and polarities of this historical societal type and its epoch: the class issue, the antagonism between labor and capital or between culture and its material basis, social movements and parties, ethnic differences, the nation-state, the welfare state, and so forth. This is the framework in which sociology developed, and, although I cannot prove it in this brief exposition, I think sociology feels obligated to this framework even where it has advanced into the abstract, generalizable realm of the "conditions for the possibility of society."

Particularly since World War II, sociology has been conceived of as the "philosophy of industrial society," as Anthony Giddens and Walter Bühl independently show.[2] If one opens up this historical line (and I can't really do that here), then it is interesting to ask what it is that conceptions of bourgeois society disassociate themselves from. For instance Saint-Simon characterized "society," in clear opposition to the unproductive nobility, as "the totality and union of those people who devote themselves to useful occupations."[3] He equates the rise of bourgeois society with the development of labor, which, and this is also relevant here, transforms the resources of nature into social values, into commodities. The abstraction from nature, its alleged availability and consumability in processes of labor and production, is thus the prerequisite of the developing bourgeois society and of its special discipline, sociology.

One can run through the possibilities for variation and controversy that may exist within this framework, and one will find that this has all actually been brought up, debated, and worked out: the theory of functional differentiation, the controversies between "material" and "cultural" perspectives, crisis theory and systems theory, the loss of the subject, theories of action—everything can be located here. Even the controversies over the future hold fast to this framework and remain within it. Postindustrialism is conceived along the lines of the production-sector mode—as a shift in domination from the industrial to the service sector. That's all. To be sure, the debate on postindustrialism, that is, on the service economy, stimulated much research. The central institutions of industrial society, however—technology and science, the professional character of labor, the class character of society—are held constant. The principles of industrialism have only come into question with the rise of postmodernity. But, at least in its French origins, the debate excludes the ecological issue and is committed more to aesthetics.

II

Such a brief and pointed presentation could give the impression that what I am going to say here is too simple and sweeping, but I think it is basically valid: well into the 1970s, sociology played out and fought for the range of variants framed by bourgeois industrial society, capitalism, and late capitalism. Since the 1980s, however, increasingly intense debates in sociological theory and in many special sociological fields have erupted concerning whether thinking and researching in categories of linear social change can be retained or whether they must be supplemented or replaced by more complex models of nonlinear, reflexive

change. Reflexivity in this connection means the modernization *of* industrial society, not *in* industrial society—that is, the detraditionalization
and reorganization of its categories, institutions, and functional principles. In this sense, the Frankfurt Sociologists' Convention in 1968
raised the issue of the "modernization of modern societies." I should
now like to indicate briefly where and how an increasing concern with
ecology has begun in sociology, so that I can subsequently show in
greater detail what perspectives I see for my own work.

Anyone who examines the sociological contribution to the ecological debate is well-advised to discard the restrictive spectacles of the
specialist and to don instead those of the social sciences. Much has
happened in the critique of ecological policy, nationally, internationally, and in the intertwining of various subnational levels of politics.
Environmental law in all its facets and foundations is still being debated; similarly, the volumes on the relationship between the economy
and ecology or between the social market economy and threats to the
environment are filling up libraries. The "ecological reconstruction of
industrial society" frequently means, first of all, a reconstruction of
the economy (ecological taxes, levies, and prices). Systems theory, in
particular, has advanced far ahead, having opened a path for sociology to the ecological issue through various innovations, such as its
inclusion of chaos and turbulence theories from the natural sciences.
Social-scientific attitude research has reconstructed and documented
the consciousness-raising process and the continuing urgency of the
ecological issue in the Western European welfare states and in the
United States.

Ecology does not always mean ecology. Sociology began quite early
with the so-called human ecology research of the Chicago school, which
is associated with the names Park and Burgess. Early in the century,
something quite different was meant by and pursued under the concept of human ecology, namely, an urban sociology inspired by Simmel's
concept of social space. "Ecological socialization research," which has
been a topic of discussion for some years, intends to include regional
points of view in socialization research. Thus the new prominence of
the concept of ecology sometimes arouses false hopes. This applies also,
for instance, to so-called electoral sociology and ecological psychology.

What has been left out in all this? Where is the blind spot of a
sociology that takes on the ecological issue? In my view, the socioeconomic and sociocultural conflict dynamics have not yet been sufficiently
deciphered. To put it in classical terms, an ecological analysis of social
structure is lacking because the old analysis, which conceives and
researches social inequalities in the categories of commodity and

prosperity production and distribution, can only grasp part of the social-structural conflict dynamics of modern societies. "Threats to nature" are no longer just threats to nature; instead, pointing them out also threatens property, capital, jobs, trade-union power, and the economic basis of entire sectors and regions. There are always losers, but there are also generally winners from public definitions of hazards, which must therefore be understood as an essential means in the competition for market shares and labor market positions.

To put it differently, an important difference from the familiar antagonism of capital versus labor lies in the fact that risk definitions split the economic camps. Latent polarizations within capital come out, and hence polarizations within labor, all the way into management, the trade unions, and the professions. It is not at all easy to discern where and how these polarizations run and how they take concrete form—organizationally and sociologically.

Another difference from the old industrial conflict is the fact that formerly something *positive* was at stake: profits, prosperity, or market share. In the new ecological conflict, by contrast, the object of contention is something *negative*: losses, destruction, threats. The ecological conflict is a "negative sum game of collective self-damage";[4] a game, then, between losers, who refuse to admit the damage, who shrug it off and repress it. That is why the connection between threat, knowledge of the threat, action and consciousness is so difficult to decipher. The sectors threatened in ecological conflict tourism, for instance— would bring about their own economic demise by admitting the threat, so that at least in the beginning their representatives become embittered opponents of the ecological movement, of public reporting on damages, and so on.

Several questions have not been sufficiently addressed: How does the ecological issue become "culturally significant" (in Max Weber's sense)? What makes it socially and politically explosive? What brings about the peculiar vacillation by the populace among indifference, cynicism, and hysteria? How are the ecological issue and the social issue related? And how, then, must the perspective on society change in order to make the ecological issue comprehensible in its cultural, social, and political dynamics?

I should like to sketch two lines of argument on this, inquiring first into the conditions for sociocultural resonance to the ecology issue, and, second, into the conditions for institutional attentiveness to it.

III

According to a widely held view, environmental consciousness and environmental policy develop as a reaction to the increased destruction of nature and the strain on the environment in industrial society. Thus, in the words of Martin Jänicke and Harald Mönch, it is "almost a banality to say: environmental policy did not come into being as a noble idea anywhere in the world. Everywhere it is the product of incalculable, generally worsening, strains on the environment."[5]

Niklas Luhmann also views sociocultural perception as a function of exposure: "In very diverse ways contemporary society sees itself afflicted again by effects that it itself set off in the environment. . . . People are not only noticing that society is changing its milieu, but also that in doing so it is undermining the conditions for its own continued existence. The problem itself is by no means new; it already appeared in very early stages of social development, but not until today does it achieve an intensity which forces itself on human communication as a continuous 'background noise'."[6]

In that view, it is the increasing destruction that forces us to pay attention. I will call this the naturalistic explanation. A number of findings argue against it. The French sociologist of technology, Philipe Roqueplo, has demonstrated that scientific involvement with the phenomenon of acid rain reaches very far back, even to the late-nineteenth century, and that it has been observed and recorded throughout the twentieth century, particularly by Swedish researchers.[7] Though pollution from acid rain increased continuously, neither the complaints of the scientists nor the scientific meetings they organized to make the complaints public were able to find a public echo. All this changed abruptly in the 1980s in Germany, after the media adopted the issue and used images and stories to raise into public consciousness a connection that had been invisible to direct perception. Subsequently, attention declined somewhat, although it remains high.

This is not a unique case. As Volker von Prittwitz shows, smog pollution was at its highest in the 1960s in Germany, and has been declining since then. By the time there were air pollution alerts in early 1979 and repeatedly during the 1980s the level of pollution had declined, and it continues to do so.

Von Prittwitz also documents the opposite situation—the greater the exposure, the fewer are the protective measures—as is the political reactions following Chernobyl: "At relatively low radiation exposures the relatively severe action criteria for radiation protection applied; when the exposures sharply increased, the radiation protective measures were drastically weakened or completely set aside."[8] If in addition one makes an *intercultural* comparison of European and Third World evaluations and perceptions of the same threat or damage, it becomes clear that parts of the ecology movement have been taken in by a naturalistic misunderstanding: it is not damage that forces protest; on the contrary, damage and protest seem to be independent. *Cultural norms and cultural willingness to perceive* decide which damage is accepted and which is not.

Why don't the Germans just say, "The forest is dying, hurrah! The Neanderthal is extinct, and so are the dinosaurs, but the world doesn't break into laments over them. Devastated forests, fields, and lakes— what a market for a forward-looking industrial policy! The replacement of nature—now that would stimulate demand, and what an export hit!"

In analytical terms, devastation and protest are isolated from each other by the cultural willingness to accept the devastation. This acceptance can be based on the pursuit of some higher value (for instance, freedom or war), on other priorities (such as increasing wealth), or in simple ignorance. It can also be based in the abstractness and omnipresence of threats, against which individual resistance is virtually impossible. As the psychologist Weinert has shown, subjective perception and the availability of alternatives play an important role in initiating activity. The willingness to accept has many bases, old and new, some deriving from traditional ways of life and some resulting from the bombardment with apocalyptic visions.[9]

The toleration of devastation erodes, if at all, only where people see themselves threatened within their own horizon in a way that they find is perceptible and meaningful. Only someone who asks what possibilities for action are open to the threatened people can appreciate why those worst affected fight so bitterly against insight into their condition. The spark of protest does not ignite among the most threatened, for whom poverty has joined filth, noise, and risk in an iron alliance of threat. Protest begins in the majority in the middle— sociologists speak of radicalized middle classes—whose norms of health and safety have been nurtured through participation in affluence, property, and education. These middle classes now see themselves threatened by ecological destruction, threatened with the loss of the fruits of their labor—leisure, relaxation, garden, home and following a rule of thumb of political sociology, alarm bells ring in the political system when the social middle feels threatened.

Cultural outrage selects among the "objectively" most urgent urgencies, and this selection is not guided by the damage but by cultural symbols and mass-media information. A comparison between France and Germany illustrates this: Early in the 1980s the major Paris newspapers declared that "Le Waldsterben" [forest destruction, literally "death of the forest"] was a fabrication that the German automobile manufacturers were using to displace their competitors in future markets.

Devastation and protest are symbolically mediated. To put it in the language of sociological theory, the systems-theoretical or the political economic view of the ecological issue requires an interactionist or phenomenological supplement and correction. In the abstractness of the devastation initiated and maintained by advanced risk industrialism, tangible symbols attain a crucial significance. They set off alarms in cultural nerves: the forest in Germany, breakfast eggs in England.

In ecological protest, then, we are dealing with a phenomenon of intrasocial sensibility and institutional attentiveness, and against this background the devastation of nature is experienced as a cultural and political alarm process and becomes the object of social actions and protests.

It is not the devastation of nature that represents the cultural sounding box for ecological alarm, but the endangering of a certain cultural design of nature, a design that refers to the conditions of welfare-state life in the center of Europe. One must inquire into the nature utopias that are gaining social importance and commitment along with the environmental movement, but not as a result of it. The assumption that the "pressure of problems" explains ecological consciousness and determines environmental policy remains unsatisfactory (nor is it asserted anywhere in pure form). Ecological sensibility and the willingness to protest are certainly influenced by many factors: population density; degree of industrialization; level of prosperity, bureaucracy, and security; the rules of democracy; and, not least, by the techno-economic resources to confront environmental damage, that is, by, winners' interests; but they are also influenced simply by cultural norms and ways of life.

Ecological consciousness is *not* nature consciousness at all but rather an intramodern, post-traditional horizon of meaning and expectation, for which—in contrast to talk of the seemingly natural nature, two things are characteristic. The first is a high degree of scientization. Perceiving an ecological crisis is only possible if, for instance, chemical formulas become "forms of experience" in the Kantian sense, historical a prioris, which therefore determine everyday perception. The second is a fading of the certainties of industrial society: class-based cultures, status milieus, and gender roles, but also national values and identities. The talk of risk is a substitute for morality, and it is gaining importance with the loss of tradition. Now one can rely on smog mortality rates, where one previously had to interpret the categorical imperative.

IV

So much—in—brief for the conditions of sociocultural resonance. Now I will turn to the conditions of institutional attentiveness. Social resonance and institutional attentiveness mutually influence one another, so that they must be viewed in context.

How can institutional attentiveness to ecological effects be deciphered sociologically? Here the concept of *risk* is essential, risk understood as *calculable, decision-based insecurity*. Institutional attentiveness is calculated from the rules that govern how one deals with self-produced consequences and damage. A double differentiation seems important here.

Human dramas—plague, natural catastrophes and famines, the threatening power of gods and demons—may or may not equal the destructive potential of developed industrial society in their deadly consequences or their measurable risk content. They are fundamentally different from industrial risks, in my sense, in that they are not the result of decisions, or more precisely, of decisions that focus on techno-economic advantages and opportunities and accept risks as merely the downside of progress. This is my first point: risks presume industrial decisions and considerations of utility. They are distinguished from war damage by their "normal birth," blessed by the guarantors of law and order, and from preindustrial natural catastrophes by their origin in decision-making. Closely connected to this second criterion are the factors of avoidability and alternatives. These factors are precisely where the political content of risks resides, for risks can no longer be blamed on something external such as God, or nature. Accountability, avoidability, and responsibility constitute risks.

Industrial capitalism is a continually risky enterprise, which people do not enter blindly. They have a very subtle system at their command for making the unpredictable predictable. The system works with accident statistics; it guarantees insurance protection, disaster protection, and medical care; and it takes care of all sorts of technical security measures. The basic idea of all these calculations and institutions is simply: precautionary after-care.

As the French sociologist François Ewald has demonstrated in detailed theoretical and historical studies, the "invention" of the risk insurance calculus lies in the industrial system's ability to act with regard to its own unpredictable future—with the help of accident scenarios and through the ability to generalize both liability rules and the principle of damage for money. A system of rules for social accountability, compensation and precaution creates present-day security in the face of an open, uncertain future.[10]

This is where the second distinction begins, the distinction between controllable consequences (risks) and uncontrollable consequences (threats) *within* industrialism. I suggest that the basis of the distinction can be taken from the institutionalized calculus of risk itself. The measures for the "rational" control of results are to the unleashed consequences what a bicycle brake is to a jetliner. The basic concepts of risk management in science, law, and politics—accident prevention, insurance protection, polluter-pays principle, liability, and so on— become ineffective in an era of chemical and genetic technology, in the face of effects that, unlike mining disasters or other occupational accidents of the early industrial age, can no longer be limited (spatially, temporally, or socially), calculated, and appropriately compensated. We know that not all the victims of Chernobyl have even been born, five years afterward! The dimensions of such events destroy the conditions for applying the accident concept and, with them, the basis for calculating and compensating for industrial consequences and damage.

Is there an operational criterion for distinguishing between risks and threats? Yes indeed: the denial of private insurance protection. This criterion accomodates nuclear energy as well as large portions of the chemical and genetic technology industries. The litmus test for uncontrollability is the lack of insurance protection.

To argue in systematic terms, nuclear, chemical, and ecological threats destroy the four principal pillars of insurance. First of all, in the face of non-illimitable, global, and often irreparable damages, the concept of financial compensation fails. Second, anticipatory after-care is out of the question for the worst imaginable accidents; the concept of security of anticipating control of consequences fails. Third, the "accident" loses its boundaries in space and time; it becomes an "accident" with a definite beginning but without an end. This means that the bases for calculation and compensation become false. Fourth and finally, because of their complexity and cross-linking, the damages and effects can only rarely be accounted for according to the principles of strict causality and individual guilt. The result is that causal accountability and jurisprudence based on the polluter-pays principle do not function.

What are the consequences for the political dynamics of the ecological issue? The environmental problem is by no means a problem of our *environs*. It is a crisis of industrial society itself, reaching deeply into the foundations of institutions; risks are industrially produced, economically externalized, juridically individualized, and scientifically legitimized. Security degenerates into mere technical safety. The secret of the calculus of risk, however, is the cooperation of technical and social standards: accountability, compensation, anticipatory after-care. When these concepts can't apply, social or political safety must be guaranteed exclusively by an increase of technical prowess.

On the other hand, entire industrial branches are operating beyond insurability, in the center of Europe, in a milieu of highly developed standards for safety and highly developed bureaucracies to implement them. A society attuned to safety and health from head to toe is confronted with the shock of risks that slip through all the loopholes of technology, law, and politics. These are the salient points of socioeconomic conflict dynamics not the scientific diagnosis of the threat as such. State industrial authority's technically centered claim to control shatters against the combination of publicized disasters, near-disasters, creeping devastation, and threats to health, legalized through institutional rationality.

Risk and insurance go hand in hand with the decay of feudal, organic communities, with the liberation and autonomization of the individual. "Risk societies" in this general sense arise through a *radicalization of modernity*, in the degree to which the traditional cognitive and physical infrastructure of industrial society melts away and everything is transformed into decisions. In the limiting case, it is impossible to avoid risk in those instances where even indecision and inaction become risky, where the multifarious risks compete with each other. This applies both to personal decisions and to technical, political, and economic decisions. "Leading one's life like an enterprise," writes Ewald, "has become since the eighteenth century the principle of a morality whose cardinal virtue is anticipation."[11] Calculating a risk means disciplining the future. Risk is the opposite side of increasing options.

Opposing this general concept, I have attempted to sketch out a second, specific concept of risk society; "risk society" in this specific sense arises only where the foundation, risk and insurance, has been disconnected. Viewed this way, the political dynamism of the ecological issue is not a function of the advancing devastation of nature; rather it arises from the facts that, on the one hand, institutions claim to provide control and security falls short and, on the other hand, in the same way, devastation is normalized and legalized, becoming an explosive problem of welfare-state policy.

V

I initially listed the reservations that impede sociology's access to the ecological issue. Then I traced where and how sociology is beginning to rise to the challenges. In the main section, I showed where I see access possibilities and working perspectives. I can clarify my approach again in a double delimitation. In specialized discussion and the public sphere, there are two competing approaches: a scientific-naturalist perception of threat and a cultural-relativist perception of threat. My approach lies between these two positions, and places the institutional handling of industrially produced challenges in the center.

The technical diagnosis of threats fails to acknowledge the cultural and symbolic mediation of the consciousness of threat. The conclusion could be, in sociological terms, social construction and sociological reconstruction of social and public diagnoses of threats.

The cultural-relativistic diagnosis fails to acknowledge that there are historically different types of risks and threats, and that this typology can be developed on the criteria of industrial risk calculation itself. The key to preventing devastation of the environment lies essentially in the institutional regulatory system, which has become historically questionable. Without sociology the ecological issue remains socially blind; with ecology the social issue becomes blind to history. However, a sociology that applies its experience of the structurability of society, which it gained in the social issue, can go beyond an ideological critique in opposing the politically dangerous confusion of society and nature. The welfare state is the first consequence of these experiences. Sociology could bring out these experiences through research on the ecological issues and argue them publicly. I will close by mentioning a few political consequences.

I am disturbed by the question of what would happen if ecological-threat industrialism were to collapse like Stalinism. (I know that is out of the question—but so was the collapse of the Eastern bloc.) What would happen if people marched through the streets after the next great accident shouting, "We are the people! Down with threats!"

If the Green Party program was taken seriously, the slogan would be: "Shut down! Stop! Smaller! Slower!" Behind all the variety in detail, the political tendency amounts to asceticism.

If the Christian Democrats were taken seriously, they would install a valve after the next maximum credible accident and a second Ministry of the Environment would be established: one for information and another for information about the information. One must distinguish the two clearly. The Social Democrats would probably demand tax increases and wave their arms.

That is perhaps a caricature. But it is important that we finally reflect on and debate the compatibility of ecology and democracy. How can more freedom, more democracy, a radicalization of modernity, and more environmental protection be possible? What would a Green modernity or an ecological democracy look like?

Allow me to present some very tentative aspects of this in closing.

First, large segments of the industries of the future will operate beyond the limit of insurability. Perhaps we should introduce the engineers, who credit reactor technology and genetic technology with almost no risk, to the insurance experts, who are apparently missing out on this immense business with no risk. Just to demand the most obvious things, the sort of things we require from any passenger-car driver, would put the industries of the future into the most embarrassing position. My first demand is therefore very modest: equality with cars! Private insurance for everyone! All industries and all research!

Second, even something this obvious is becoming an unreachable utopia in risk society. I would therefore like to add a few demands. Like the "social question" in the nineteenth century, the "ecological question" today must be related to changes in institutions (legal norms). There was no clear answer to the question of causality for factory or occupational accidents in the nineteenth century either. Did the worker cause the accident by sticking his (now-separated) arm into the machine? Is the engineer who designed the machinery the cause? Perhaps it was the entrepreneur who was turning the screw for higher production? Causality always remains ambiguous, if only for scientific reasons. The accountability problem had to be and—even in the social area—still has to be settled by agreements worked out in conflict, that is, social agreements, legal standards must be regulated. These historical experiences must be transferred to the ecological question. That implies, for instance:

1. Establishing correlation standards as the foundation for the legal recognition of damage, instead of strict causal proof, which, given the global interdependence of threat production, can only be produced in exceptional cases;

2. Changing the burden of proof, so that the agents in industry and the sciences become obligated to justify themselves in public;

3. Responding to claims of technical safety with liability for damages;

4. Reformulating the polluter-pays principle by creating regional accountabilities for benefitted and harmed business sectors: for instance, coastal regions, with their hotel and restaurant structure, and the chemical and industrial regions, which create the pollutant muck that drives away guests;

5. Suggesting and negotiating agreements on the recognition of damage and on compensation payments between a region's industrial plants and its population (as is sometimes done in Japan).

I will conclude with a few verses from Hans Magnus Enzensberger:[12]

Even the end of the world
is perhaps
only provisional
For the time being, we die
calmly
in our chaise longues
Then we'll see what happens.

Notes

1. J. F. Short, "The Social Fabric at Risk," *American Sociological Review* 49 (1984): 711–725.
2. Giddens, "Die klassische Gesellschaftstheorie und der Ursprung der modernen Soziologie," in Wolf Lepenies, ed., *Geschichte der Soziologie*, vol. 1, (Frankfurt: Suhrkamp, 1981): Bühl, "Das ökologische Paradigma in der Soziologie," in H. Niemeyer, ed., *Soziale Beziehungsgeflechte* (Berlin, 1980), 102.
3. Saint-Simon, in F. Kool and W. Krause, eds., *Die frühen Sozialisten* (Olden und Freiburg, 1967).
4. Claus Offe, "Die Chancen der Risikogesellschaft," in U. Beck, ed., *Politik in der Risikogesellschaft* (Frankfurt: Suhrkamp, 1991), 216.
5. M. Jänicke and H. Mönch, "Ökologischer und wirtschaftlicher Wandel im Industrieländervergleich," in M. G. Schmidt, ed., *Staatstätigkeit: International und historisch vergleichende* (Opladen: Analyse, 1988).
6. Niklas Luhmann, *Ökologische Kommunikation* (Opladen: Westdeutscher Verlag, 1986), 11–12.
7. Philipe Roqueplo, "Der saure Regen: Ein Unfall in Zeitlupe," *Soziale Welt* 4 (1986): 402–426.
8. Volker von Prittwitz, *Das Katastrophen-Paradox* (Opladen, 1991).
9. Weinert, *Individuelle, gesellschaftliche und staatliche Bewertung des Risikos* (Akademie der Wissenschaften zu Berlin, Forschungsbericht 2, Umweltstandart, Grundlagen Tatsachen und Bewertungen am Beispiel des Strahlenrisikos, 1992).
10. F. Ewald, *Der Vorsorgestaat* (Frankfurt: Suhrkamp Verlag, 1993).
11. Ibid., 220.
12. Enzensberger, "Gedankenflucht," in *Zukunftsmusik* (Frankfurt: Suhrkamp Verlag, 1991), 80–81.

11

The Conflict of
Two Modernities

Sociology is the answer. But what was the question? Is sociology as we practice it, with its theories and controversies, perhaps the answer to the *social issue?* Then is it not time to ask, How can society be an answer to the ecological issue?

Asking it a different way, Does the funeral dirge for Marxism, now being publicly celebrated with good justification and bad manners, obscure the obsolescence of the Western sociology of modernization?

In order to interpret the theme of the sociologists' 1968 Frankfurt convention—"the modernization of modern societies"—I would like to propose a theoretical distinction that allows us to open up sociology to the challenges of industrial development on the basis of its own conceptual foundations: the distinction between primary and reflexive modernization. Primary modernization means the rationalization of tradition, while reflexive modernization means the rationalization of rationalization.

To date, modernization has always been conceived of, by delimitation from the world of traditions and religions, as a liberation from the constraints of unrestrained nature. What happens if industrial society becomes a "tradition" to itself? What if its own necessities, functional principles and fundamental concepts are undermined, broken up and demystified with the same ruthlessness as were the supposedly eternal truths of earlier epochs?

This is the text of the address with which I opened the Convention of German Sociologists in 1990 at Frankfurt am Main.

133

The rationalization of rationalization is a key topic in the wake of the end of the East-West conflict and in view of the global challenges of industrial civilization. I would like to pick out three questions to test the viability of this concept: (1) How does the face of industrial society change in reflexive modernization? (2) How can sociology be opened up to the ecological issue? (3) To what extent do primary and reflexive modernization represent poles of social conflict in Germany and Europe after the Cold War?

I

What society are we living in? In a society in which everything that was conceived of as belonging together is being drawn apar—industrial production without industrial society. Industrial society, understood as a model of the lifeworld in which gender roles, nuclear families and classes are interlocked, is disappearing, while the engine of industrial dynamism continues to run, or, rather, *because* of the running engine of industrial dynamism. The same mode of production, the same political system, the same dynamics of modernization are producing a different society in the lifeworld: different networks, different circles of relationships, different lines of conflict, and different forms of political alliances for individuals. How is that possible? Key concepts and variables of industrial society—class, nuclear family, and occupation— were fragmented and shuffled into new patterns by the expansion of the welfare state following World War II, by the expansion of education, by increasing real wages, and by social and geographical mobility, as well as by increases in women's work outside the home, in divorce rates, and in the flexibility of paid labor.

This perspective contains three theses.

First, industrial society as a *systematic context*, that is, the dynamism of business, politics, and science, is dissolving industrial society as a *context of experience*. People are being freed from the certainties and standardized roles of industrial society. Men are no longer automatically fathers, fathers no longer the sole wage earners, and sole wage earners often no longer husbands. In earlier generations social stratum, income, profession, spouse, and political attitude were generally a unified whole; today this biographical package is disintegrating into its components. For instance, income is no longer an automatic indicator of place and type of residence, marital status, political behavior and so on.

Second, modern society is splitting *into* on the one hand, *inside* the institutions that preserve the old certainties and normalcies of industrial society, and, on the other, a variety of lifeworld realities that are moving further and further from those images. To paraphrase Brecht, political parties and labor unions may soon find themselves forced to discharge their voters and members, who are no longer willing to conform to the institutionalized image of themselves.

Third, a double problematic results. More and more people are slipping through the normalized gaps in the social safety network (for example, poverty is made inevitable by working conditions so uncertain that wages fall below the eligibility threshold for social insurance). In addition, the institutions of the lifeworld and the consensus through which they once maintained their existence no longer apply (consider the rise of swing voters and opinion-poll democracy). This amounts to something I like to call the "individualization of institutions," for it is no longer possible to conceive of institutions independent of individuals. Conflicts *over* institutional policy break out *within* the institutions.

Industrial production without industrial society: even in its preliminary form, this developmental variant is slippery. Any variation, even any independent variation, of industrial society as a systematic *and* an experiential context is analytically closed off in sociological theory. Marx conceived of industrial society *as* a class society. Capitalism *without* classes is not just a betrayal, it is tantamount to trying to jump out the window and fly upward. Parsons, on the other hand, categorized capitalism as a nuclear-family society. The dissolution of gender hierarchies violates the *good manners* of functional prerequisites.

"Adieu to class society" to many, this sounds as if class society has been overcome. Since no one can seriously claim that, however, in view of the continued existence of social hierarchy, we remain unable to understand the developmental variant that is being considered here, that is, an alteration of the social structure of social inequality that can easily accompany an increase in social inequality, as the increasing gap in incomes in the Federal Republic over the past few years attests.

"Adieu" also suggests dissolution. Where the nuclear family is concerned, all joking stops. People get caught in religious and political taboos, and, not least important, in defending their own private world structures.

I have no intention of covering up the balancing necessary here, but only of pointing out the awkward beginning. Since variation in the basic pattern of the lifeworld is politically and sociologically disallowed, alternative typologies for sociostructural organization in the lifeworld are in practice either nonexistent or rudimentary. Beyond the industrial world structures of class, stratum, and nuclear family, there is only a loose collection of individuals rustling in the wind.

Let me give a comparison: The theory of industrial society posits various production sectors, and so it is possible to thoroughly explore, work out, and discuss the effects of a change of priorities from an industrial to a service society. But, in the case of social structures, there are no anthropological, moral, or political alternatives. As long as this is so, even empirical research is stuck in its well-worn groove. The abundant doubts, ambiguities, and deviations, the entire fog of the social structure, shows up in masses of data that are repeatedly poured into the old categorical bottles. But the diagnosis of continuity when there is no theoretical alternative is empty, not falsifiable.

Consider, for example, research about the nuclear family. There have been radical changes in family structure: cohabitation, informal marriages, exponential increases in the number of single-person households, single parents. Yet, with a few important exceptions, family sociology, especially in Germany, has been busy for years signalling "all clear." In the heart of the nuclear family, everything is apparently completely healthy!

We're forced to ask whether German family sociology is wedded to the nuclear family. What must happen for empirical sociology to even consider the possibility of a conceptual reform of its research field? I am certain that even when 70 percent of the households in large cities are single-person households, a point that is not very far away, our intrepid family sociologists will have millions of bits of data to prove that those 70 percent are only living alone because they used to live in nuclear families or that they will do so again some day. And if you ask me (I know you cannot, so I will ask myself) why the nuclear family is so stable in Germany, then I will give you my secret answer: because family sociology is so faithful about inquiring into it! Because there is no typology, neither in social statistics nor sociologically, whose core is not the nuclear family.

One can imagine-and-discuss at least the following alternatives to the traditional nuclear family:

- The entire familial structure is underdifferentiated: that is, not one family, but families.
- Primary relationships fluctuate, along a variety of paths, between the nuclear family and other ways of life.
- Parenthood is divisible; therefore divorce multiplies parenthood— physical and social parenthood diverge; children have many parents; kinship networks become multiple and ambivalent.
- High remarriage rates testify to the continuing attractiveness of the nuclear family, but they are only as high as they are because of the frequency of divorce, and high remarriage rates maximize the number of parents and grandparents. New postfamilial, autofamilial, and

exofamilial networks emerge; behind the facade of the momentary and superficial nuclear family, each individual family member is a member of many families.[1]

The suspicion that the continuity of the nuclear family has its real basis in the continuity of nuclear family *research*, is corroborated by parallels from research into German social structure. The alternative to classes was strata. Strata, like classes, are large groups, conceived in terms that are politically paler and less significant. They offer, how-ever, the same metaphor of a social structure as a torte, only with more layers and more frosting. Here too, the constancy of the typologies and conceptual schemata is taken to mean that the data are constant, and all of them together are taken to mean that the social structure is constant. And if we do not just ignore this type of sociology, we will still be living in this society of nuclear family, class, professions and industry three hundred years from now.

It is also possible, however, to turn the tables on the structural tra-ditionalists. In an empirical stalemate the better theory will dominate. On a closer look, we see that what is being extended into all eternity under the name "modern society" is actually a hybrid between feudal and industrial society. Homemaking, for instance, as I have learned from women's studies, supports paid labor; it is its backrest and sup-porting rear leg, so to speak. Both forms of labor arose in comple-mentary fashion and with opposing principle, in the phase of primary industrialization. Homemaking means not having any money of one's own, but also not having any pressure to meet a quota; instead one has people, large and small, screaming for attention around the clock. Certainly it is an indispensable labor, which adheres to women through birth, specifically for having been born female, and through love, or, more precisely, through marriage; it is as permanent as it is unpaid and uninsured. Such a thing can hardly be stable in a milieu of in-creasing options and market-based individualization. Thus threads of industrial countermodernity extend through the tissue of the old in-dustrial society: let us have universalism, of course, but only up to national and gender boundaries please; let us have freedom to decide and democracy, certainly, but not, please, in key questions of technology and science.

The collapse of Stalinism has again drawn attention to the fact that a social system's claim to be an independent agent depends upon one central condition: the consent of individuals to its autonomy. I say "again" because Hannah Arendt had already made it clear, on the basis of a bitter real-life example, that bureaucracies only become machines

through the conscious, or sometimes semi-conscious, culturally mediated efforts of people. Her example was an international intercultural
comparison of the bureaucratic organization of the annihilation of the
Jews in all its individual steps—rounding up, separating, deporting
and so forth. She showed that the bureaucratic machinery that operated
so perfectly in Germany was sabotaged in Italy by a traditional aversion to bureaucracy, and was spectacularly sabotaged in Denmark, where
members of the royal family and many citizens chose to wear the Star
of David. It was slowed in Bulgaria by spontaneous demonstrations of
sympathy from the population, while in Rumania it ran almost more
smoothly than in Germany.[2] Postwar German sociology has never acknowledged this lesson.

The autonomy of social systems is culturally borrowed. It was possible to forget this so long as the basic forms of the society of the individuals and institutional society still corresponded. When the two societies
diverged, the last grand, central illusion of sociology decays: the meta-
physics of social systems. Class, nuclear family, marriage, profession,
female role, male role, the forms and formulas of consensus, all crumble. The social molds that political parties and organizations use to
build their programs and their work become indistinct. The systems
of social protection, administration of work or family policy preserve
an industrial society normalcy that no longer applies for larger and
larger groups in the population. All of this means that institutions
become individual-dependent, not because the individuals have become
powerful but because the institutions have become historically
contradictory.

Sociology has so far settled the conflicts outside or on the edges of
institutions, in the overlap between "system and lifeworld" (Habermas).
In reflexive modernization, conflicts erupt *inside* the institutions over
foundations and developmental alternatives. This applies to women's
policy, transportation policy, municipal policy, corporate labor and
employment policy, and technology policy, among others. The cultural
basis that allows a system to be autonomous is a relic of pre-democratic
and, in that sense, premodern ways of life. The stimulation of democracy brings that confusion and quarreling that is testified to by such
diverse phenomena as individual-centered management strategies, concern for business ethics, self-critical lawyers and doctors, feminist professional organizations and many others.

Reflexive modernization deprives commonalities—from the tribal
organization to social systems—of their bases. As a thought experiment, it was possible to predict what is now becoming a problem for
thought and policy making. Modernization is a dissolution process; its

result is that social standards, from tradition to the categorical imperative, only receive lip service. This does not mean the end of all community, as cultural criticism has been lamenting for over a century now, but the end of all prescribed, retrievable, and predictable community and the beginning of a new type. This new type of community no longer rules from the top down, nor can it be poured into people through the funnel of the functionalist model of socialization. Instead, it must be waited for, won, fought out, invented and negotiated from below. The question arises in response, How is society possible as a social movement of individuals?

II

What does the ecological question mean in this connection? Might it not be wiser for a sociologist to keep silent on some question or other? Where is the guarantee that the ecology issue itself will not dissolve into oblivion at the next turn of the *Zeitgeist*, so that we late converts to ecology would be conducting research without a research subject, or worse, without research funding? Where is the hard core of the ecological issue? What forces or justifies sociological competence beyond moral support and appeals, which are of course open to everyone.

Industrial society is an industrial *production* society. In its development it produces an industrial *consequence* society, its oversized and negative mirror image in everything: pattern, autodynamism, interest, valency, conflict logic, and hysteria. Before, there were prosperity, property, business, the nation-state, social protection; now there are only unappetizing and unpleasant things that no one wants, things that encounter denial and defensiveness and that must be classified by what they gnaw at: health, life, property, markets, confidence; things that have local dimensions, but that also have international ones, ignoring all the class and system borders of industrial society. Here, too, there is inequality; poverty attracts risks. But the inequalities diminish in the global surplus of risks. Pollutants do not spare the drinking water of directors general.

One could say that this is all nebulous, that it sounds like late Shakespeare. But struggles over how to dispose of things dominate transportation policy and the location of waste incinerators is not only reaching into chemical and biotechnical laboratories but also affecting food policy, water policy, air policy, and agriculture policy. These struggles cause world markets to collapse, threaten entire industries and recreation areas, and create in the population an unstable mood between cynicism and hysteria. In other words: the universal shadow of modernity, the world society of consequences, thwarts the old industrial order. Today, a sociology that looks the other way here is a sociology of the past; it no longer understands the society it investigates.

I would like to lay out this assessment in three theses.

First, the model of industrial society conceives of things as being together that are now breaking apart and developing in contrary ways: industrial production society and industrial consequence society. This presumes a distinction between controllable consequences, *risks*, and uncontrollable consequences, *threats*, in industrialism. The criteria for the distinction can be derived from the institutionalized regulatory system itself. The standards that "rationally" control side effects have become largely ineffectual. In the chemical and atomic age, all the fundamental concepts of risk management in business, law, and politics—including the concepts of accident, insurance protection, the polluter-pays principle, liability, and the like—fail in the face of consequences and devastation that can no longer be limited spatially, temporally, and/or socially, as could early industrial operating and occupational accidents; nor can they be appropriately calculated and compensated for. Technically, the probability of occurrence may be minimized by the appropriate arrangements, but what threatens us spans generations and nations. We know that the casualties of Chernobyl have not even all been born yet. In the face of consequences of such dimensions, the concepts of accident and the calculation of and compensation for industrial consequences and devastation all fail.

Is there an operational criterion, then, for distinguishing between risks and threats? Very definitely: the denial of private insurance protection. And this applies to the whole spectrum of modern mega-technology.

The environmental problem is by no means a problem of the world surrounding us. It is a crisis of industrial society itself, deeply rooted in the foundations of its institutions and with considerable political resonance. Threats are produced industrially, externalized economically, individualized juridically, legitimized scientifically, and minimized politically. This becomes palpable in the fact that (in the best case!) everyone observes the rules, with the result that the oceans, species, and forests are dying.

The key to combating destruction of the environment is not found in the environment itself, nor in a different individual morality or in different research or business ethics; by nature it lies in the regulatory systems of the institutions that are becoming historically questionable. Without sociology, the ecological issue will remain opaque to society and impervious to action. A sociology, however, that transfers its experiences of the mutability of society which it has gained from the welfare state to the ecological issue, can do more than simply critique ideology to oppose the politically dangerous confusion of nature and society that is now spreading everywhere. Asserting that the central problem of accountability is not amenable to human intervention is simply bad sociology from the craftsman's point of view. Because the question of causality *never* provides an answer to the problem of accountability, the welfare issue could and still can only be grasped in conventions and social agreements. The problem of accountability is an issue of accountability *customs* and accountability *agreements*, hence, requiring social models that must be accepted or invented, fought for, and pushed through despite resistance. The welfare state is the first result of these experiences. Sociology can bring this experience to light again with research on the ecological crisis and argue it out in public.

My second thesis is that the industrial production society manufactures its opposite, the global society of industrial consequences, not only in the industrial/technical sense, but also in the social/sociological sense, which amounts to blanket approbation by avoiding the essential problems. Consider the example of acceptability levels.

Acceptability levels both forbid and permit. They permit whatever they do not address. Whatever is permitted is non-toxic, even if it results in permanent poisoning. Acceptability levels thus force a distinction between the permissible, which is officially detoxified (but only officially), and the toxic, which collects in oceans and abdomens. From this one law can formulate the law of the social production of threats and devastation: The less is forbidden, the more is officially non-toxic, which poses invisible and uncontrollable long-term threats. The key point is that the official verdict of non-toxicity negates the toxicity of the toxin and, thus, becomes a safe-conduct for pollution.

What Max Weber was not yet able to see, but which must concern us, is the law of modernity, changed in the course of its establishment, according to which the uncontrollability of the consequences grows with the claims to control instrumental rationality. The ecological issue is a special case of this, in which control and non-control, the nonexistence of threats and therefore their reproduction and strengthening, coincide and cooperate. We need to reconstruct the instrumental rationality theory of bureaucracy as a Potemkin theory. The administration of uncontrollable things must lead to ridiculous bureaucratic travesties. A wonderful example, fit for a collector, is the idyll of emergency management in the atomic age. Foreign nuclear reactor accidents are not counted, for administrative reasons, while domestic ones are considerate enough to limit their threats to a 29-mile radius, around the nuclear power plant. In this sense, we need to distinguish between the administration of nonsense and the administration of nonsense by nonsensical means.

My third thesis is that repressing and denying threats is a unique type of social activity. The primary industrial conflict, labor versus capital, is overlapped by a negative-sum game of collective self-damaging. Here the disputed advantages are largely exhausted in defining, warding off, and accounting for negative consequences. This war game develops its own logic, scenarios, drives forms of conflict, and typical patterns. For instance, it is necessary to defend the arrangements of manufactured unaccountability in the law, in science, and in local politics. There are times and cases where it is worthwhile to be obstructionist, and others where dramatizing others' threats whitewashes the risks of one's own products. Playing up the ozone hole, for instance, favors nuclear energy indirectly and without any biased activity on one's own part, and thus it may occasionally be appropriate to promote the protests of environmental activists whom one would otherwise oppose in the harshest terms.

Once a threat—forest destruction, for instance—has been socially recognized as such, one must at least change one's language and place one's own products and productions in the service of this great new cause. Even more, there is a rush to exploit the threat. Its causal architecture opens future markets and lays pipelines for research funding. Certainly, everything is unaccountable, multifunctional, and cross-linked beyond causality. But now this is suddenly no longer the case. Now it is time for symbolic action, and there the old monocausality prevails. In the end, the causes—of forest destruction for instance— are not trucks, not the lack of a speed limit, not coal-fired power plants; rather, following the old industrial society formula, the lack of a catalytic converter becomes the lightning rod for citizen protest. The selection of the scapegoat cannot be made and justified based on scientific data and arguments alone. Therefore it is handed to the sociology of social design on a silver platter.

The key point, however, goes far beyond this. Ecological conflict logic is not played out by different agents or different institutions in different arenas but, rather, by the same industrial society agents (supplemented by social movements and citizens' groups). The prevailing system of game rules is shuffled together with another one. People play parcheesi and blindman's bluff at the same time.

Labor unions, for instance, can find themselves involuntarily pushed onto management's side by attacks from ecological groups. Not only does their position in the next round of collective bargaining suffer from this, but also, the white collar staff that they are wooing may decide to join the management directly. The throttling of local transportation policy inflames the factional struggles within the traditional labor party, which means that the profile of the party begins to blur together with that of their conservative opponent or the Greens. Since this issue can only be constructed or destroyed within their frame of reference, scientists find themselves in the equally pleasant and embarrassing position of serving all masters, they direct the denial, determination, and removal of the threats. In general terms, the institutions' objectives become ambiguous and shady, not infrequently enriched by the other side's objective; and thus not only do their profiles and structures blur, they also become dependent on actions and individuals.

The ecological crisis is depriving institutions of the basis of their autonomy. Delegating contradictions means that one can distinguish justice from injustice and rules from pronouncements. Everything must be reinterpreted. The ecological crisis is a liberating process within and against bureaucracy. The rigidity of roles that functionalism asserts collapses in the shifting of stage sets and conflict scenarios. In one sense, the ecological crisis can be compared to the sixteenth century Peasant Revolts: The players are released from functional ties, just as the peasants were released from their ties to the liege lord. This is not an abrupt but a creeping process. Prosperity and the production of threats yield a defensive performance of what is still considered necessary rather than consent—while simultaneously constructing escape tunnels. I nearly said, as in Stalinism.

The two parts of my diagnosis fit together. In reflexive modernization, the institutions of industrial society lose their historical foundations and become contradictory, conflicted, and dependent on the individual; they prove to be in need of consent and of interpretation and open to internal coalitions and social movements. The question of the individual is raised once again, not directly but via the detour of institutional criticism. This all remains politically ambiguous, however. For instance, reflexive modernization serves not only the ecological opposition but also the opposition to that opposition. What results from it and what can be made of it remains open, and must remain open, if the theory is not to come into conflict with itself.

The theory of reflexive modernization calls the diagnostic bite of competing theories into question. It differs from crisis theories, claiming that the pressing questions are the expression of triumphs, not crises, of industrialism. It contradiction to functionalism, it asserts the self-denormalization of industrial society. In contradiction to theories of postmodernity, it insists that modernity is just beginning. And, in opposition to theories of social and ecological limits, it points to the transformation of the premises and the coordinate system of industrial modernity.

III

We postwar Germans believe unwaveringly in the compatibility of an economic boom and private political conservatism in some form or another. This very potent utopia is a kind of yodeling high-tech that attempts to fuse the day before yesterday with the day after tomorrow, perfectly and forever. If my diagnosis is correct, the modernization of modern societies, with its unleashed dynamism, is smashing this petty-bourgeois supermodernism to bits. Modernity is not a hansom cab one can get out of on the next corner if one no longer likes it, as Max Weber said, and this still applies when modernity turns the corner into reflexive application.

It is also true, however, that the rush to adopt the Western model in post-Stalinist Eastern Europe and the integration of East Germany with West Germany represent a revival of primary modernization in Germany and Europe, with hopes for the economic growth of that earlier stage; but also with the return of its nationalism and ethnic rivalries. The truth lies in conceiving of both alternatives together. The Germany that is coming into being is a Germany with *two* modernities, and it must work out a European, indeed a global, conflict within itself.

The contrasts between primary and reflexive modernization are also opening to discussion a fundamental political conflict. In all aspects of social development, the praxis of "more of the same," which drew new strength from the collapse of the Stalinist bloc, is encountering doubters and people trying to restrain its effects, people who are searching for ways to an alternative modernity.

This is becoming a personal, everyday, conflict as well as a fundamental, political one, and it is occurring on all levels: neighborhood, municipality, nation, world, with diffuse and fluctuating alliances and with no recognizable principles for compromise. The ability to tolerate, to endure insoluble contradictions, and to view the world from an opposing viewpoint has never been so urgent and, at the same time, so endangered as it is in the impending conflict of the two modernities, in which people must learn how to laugh at themselves. What is needed is self-limitation, that is, settling for imperfection.

In casting off Stalinism, "freedom," the magic word of European modernity, has taken on a new, even a German-bourgeois, sound. But the Western industrial countries are not free either. They are freer. Their claim to freedom and democracy conceals the industrial compulsion they embrace.

It has always been the same. The ancient Greeks drew the line at the slaves in their demands for equality. And slavery lasted for thousands of years: Thoreau, the master dreamer of the American Dream, was still struggling against slavery, which was defended at the time as being economically indispensable (not unlike the justifications for nuclear energy and economic expansion today). The limit for science was religion. "Human equality" was always "male equality." Just a historical moment ago, an eternal law prevailed: Democracy ends at the wall of the East-West conflict. And today, limits still prevail: self-determination and democracy, why of course, but not if it conflicts with the imperialism of technology, science, and industry.

This is central: There is no difference in principle between considering slave labor to be immutable, recognizing equality only for males, and declaring the absolute dominance of technology and the fatalistic transfiguration of ecological self-destruction.

The conflict of the future will no longer be between East and West, between communism and capitalism, but between the countries, regions and groups on the way to primary modernity and those that are attempting to relativize and reform this project self-critically, based on their experience of modernity. The conflict of the future will be the conflict of two modernities, which will battle over the compatibility of survival and human rights for all citizens of the earth. Making this conflict understandable could become an essential task for sociology.

Notes

1. Approaches to this appear in U. Beck and E. Beck-Gernsheim, *Das ganz normale Chaos der Liebe* (Frankfurt a.M., 1990; translation forthcoming from Polity Press).
2. Hannah Arendt writes: "The inexpressible cruelties of a spontaneous pogrom on a gigantic scale were too much even for the SS, in fact they gave it a bit of a scare; they intervened to stop the slaughter, so that the murder could proceed in the way they considered civilized" (*Eichmann in Jerusalem* [Munich, 1986], p. 232).

12

The Unfinished Democracy

Does NATO still exist? Have the Germans united, or reunited or been forced together? How is Gorbachev doing this morning? And what about Europe? Did it slip overnight into the crack between Asia and Africa? These are some of the things a newspaper reader looking at the world in black and white asks himself greedily and a bit uneasily every morning. And now we hear about the "victory of democracy" and the "end of history" from the other side of the Atlantic. What is that supposed to mean?

The point of this intensely controversial thesis from Francis Fukuyama, director of planning in the U.S. State Department, and therefore suspect of being involved in the geopolitical architecture of the 1990s, is that none of these spontaneous objections around the globe affect him. "The West has won the cold war," stated an invitation I recently received from the state government of Hessia to a discussion of the future. We've finally won a war! This victory orgy over the vanquished is not appropriate. Drug addiction, criminality, unemployment, poverty—the West should sweep its own step before declaring the American Way of Life the endpoint of history, was the irritated opinion of Countess Marion von Dönhoff.[1]

Fukuyama is no cowboy strategist, however. He has clambered up on the shoulders of earlier thinkers such as Hegel, Marx, and Weber to take a look into the future. He sees the events in Eastern Europe as a late victory of Hegel over Marx. Considering the democratic upheavals in Eastern Europe, it is important to rediscover the historical power of ideas. Certainly, being able to shop at fine stores has its attractions. But it was also the cry for freedom and democracy from millions of powerless people that helped to force overmilitarized totalitarianism to its knees.

147

One result, however, is that the geopolitical coordinate system, the ideological Archimidean point around that which economic and military blocs have formed since World War II, is collapsing not only in Europe but around the world. Even the winning side is losing the strength it owed to its utopianism. The Cold War is ending in a hash of universal suffrage and consumerism. What remain are conflicts over how to put together the puzzle whose parts are the free market, planning, democracy, dictatorship and socialism, in contexts that cover a spectrum ranging from Sweden to South Africa, including Eastern European contexts of liberalized socialism.

This is not the door to eternal world peace; it is more likely to be the starting gun for a resurgence of old conflicts between ethnic groups, regions, religions, and nations, perhaps even leading to war. The only history that is ending is the history that was driven by the conflict of competing visions for a better world. The losers are the dissident intellectuals, who nostalgically (nuture) their utopian visions of a "third way." And a loser, too, is Western culture, according to Fukuyama, since it will lose its historical tensions in a future of technological details.

Is this a healthy salutary realism? Or is it a glass-bead game with a thousand unknowns? Could it be that the conflict that led to Fukuyama's "end of history" already had the features of another epoch, one that will begin where the other one ends? Why does a system that was militarized down to the factory level, that for forty years, used all its power, to determine individuals' self-image and stimulate them to voluntary conformity, suddenly break down when those individuals climb over the prison bars of their own fear and demand democracy, the much abused "D" in the middle of "GDR"? This is the key question, which quickly regates all the facile interpretations standing ready.

Contrary to all the instant explanations, there is no such thing as a revolution that could start from nothing within a system of organized and surveilled conformity, a system with no organization, no instruments of powe , no copying machines or telephones, and force the rulers to self-criticism, self-reform, and self-disempowerment just by assembling in a square, and that furthermore could accomplish all this not in ten years, not in two years, but within a few days or weeks. With all due respect to reality, that is a pure fairy tale. Perhaps the overthrow of social circumstances is followed by the overthrow of our ability to think about them.

What kind of conflict are we dealing with, then, in which decades of oppression can be abolished non-violently, from one day to the next; where even the boldest dreams of those who began the rebellion are surpassed, and oppression simply flies away, muttering the words "impossible" and "out of the question."

The striking thing is, first of all, that ordinary individuals rebelled against a "system" that allegedly dominated them in even the smallest aspects of day-to-day existence. But it is not only the planned economy that is bankrupt. Systems theory, which conceives of society as independent of the subject, has also been thoroughly refuted. In a society without consensus, devoid of a legitimating core, even a single gust of wind can bring down the whole house of cards of power. The soft— people's orientations, hopes, ideas and interests of people—triumphs over the hard—the organization, the established, the powerful, the armed. Eastern Europe is one large citizens' initiative celebrating a success that is actually running it over.

The differences between exuberant citizens in East and West are obvious and have often been mentioned, but much less often mentioned is their quite considerable common ground: both are basis-oriented, extra-parliamentary, not tied to classes or parties, organizationally and programmatically diffuse and contentious. And similar, too, are the Horatio-Alger-like careers of political issues on both sides: First criminalized, opposed, ridiculed, but later included party programs and acknowledged in inaugural speeches. This is how it went with the ecological issues, the women's issue, and the peace movement, which are now being surpassed by galloping democratization in Eastern Europe.

The most socially astonishing, and probably least understood phenomenon of the 1980s, is the unexpected renaissance of subjectivity. In our case, it was the citizen's groups that put the topic of an endangered world on the political agenda against the resistance of science and established parties. There is now a universal compulsion to pay lip service to ecology, though the bad old ways go on unchanged.

In Eastern Europe, little groups of conspiratorial citizens are swelling into popular movements that are redesigning the foundation of the state. Democratic subversion has won a quite improbable victory. In Germany, this took the form of a break with an authoritarian everyday culture, whose predetermined obedience made every sort of official nonsense possible. It is striking that many of the people who now utter the word "revolution" almost with delight would otherwise consider the street to be only a gathering place for the mob.

Furthermore, events show vividly that any uprising from below gets caught by the superior strength of the bureaucracy unless it is assisted by a revolution from the top down. At the critical moment, someone in the right position must have prevented the deployment of state power against the "counter-revolution." Hungary in 1956, Czechoslovakia in 1968, and China in 1989 provide sad illustrations of attempted uprisings where the crucial intervention did not occur. No one would have guessed how much willingness to become Paul was hiding in the Communist Saul factories. Indeed what is striking is how susceptible to self-reform a Stalinistic power apparatus can be. The Gorbachevs, Jaruzelskis, Modrows, and their fellow combatants in the hierarchy may come too late and may fall victim to new waves of opposition of one type or another, but the fact remains that they are there, in a control system whose often-proclaimed perfection now proves incapable even of keeping evangelical Christians out of the centers of power.

In East Germany, there is much evidence to support the historian Lutz Niethammer's assessment that the power of the ruling Socialist Unity Party is being accelerated, because of a generational conflict, a youth revolt, which is catching up to the West Germany experience of 1968. Those who were born after the war are taking power away from the "old men," the founding generation, whose antifascist self-image long ago turned into clichés and got lost in the silence between generations. Despite the differences, there are remarkable parallels to the restlessness of citizens in the West. Let no one be deceived by the calm before the next storm of a chemical, atomic, or nuclear catastrophe. Beneath the surface of conformity ecological criticism has entered all areas of activity, not through the curriculum, not through the official door, but through the back door. It destabilizes existing routine, invisibly splits the industrial actors, in ways not yet politically tangible, all the way up to the management of the chemical industry, and not least of all because of the penetrating questions children ask their parents.

The international aspect of the revolution's dynamics stands out. Despite all our pride, the November revolution in East Germany is actually a late product of the new Democratic Internationale in Eastern Europe, and would be inconceivable without the ever present example of the Soviet Union, now that it has changed, or the civil courage of the Hungarians and the Poles. The word "freedom" has been revived in Germany as a translation of *perestroika*. And the Wall was opened by Hungary. Only the stream of refugees made possible by Hungary brought East Germans into the streets. Behind the decline of power was a kind of border-crossing general strike.

An interrelatedness that surpasses nationalities, however, also characterize the ecological crisis. If the North Sea and the Adriatic Sea die, then all the adjacent countries must clean up the poisonous muck prepared for them by the industrial regions of central Europe. The protest against this is still hampered by the knowledge that protest must reveal the conditions which make public what confirms the hopelessness of its own position. But what happens if this point is exceeded and hopelessness really does rule?

Francis Fukuyama, the Hegel in the U.S. State Department, is right. The ideological fortress mentality of the East-West conflict is dissolving. He is also wrong. It's being replaced by conflict between system and citizen, between democracy promised and democracy withheld. In the Eastern Bloc this conflict is the struggle for basic rights; and here, the conflict is for the full implementation of rights that were only granted in truncated form. The "democratic issue" has reawakened worldwide.[2]

In the late 1960s, Hannah Arendt viewed the democratic issue as the "rebellion that is spanning the globe." Its opposite, in her view, is the "no-man's rule" of bureaucracy, which causes opposition to slip into emptiness, vapidity, fundamentalism or terrorism. The visible rule of the Communist Party, by contrast, has the virtue of identifiability. For example, in the tinkering progress made in genetic engineering and human genetics and its imminent widespread application, which will certainly shake the human substance of society, there is no site for decision making and no decision maker. As yet, there is not even anything like a decision. Things worm their way through and advance here and there, tagging along as side effects of considerations that are determined on the basis of completely different priorities (career, competition, opening of markets, investments).

Fukuyama does not devote a single word to the central challenges to democracy that are provoked by the victory of the industrial system: ecology and technocracy. In both theory and practice, the question of how to democratically defuse the problem of the industrial system's production of both wealth *and* destruction remains completely open in both theory and practice.

Here lies the central task for the Europe of the future, and thus also for the growing together of the two Germanies. To borrow a distinction from Thomas Mann, will a European Germany result or a German Europe, a vision of horror outside and inside our borders or will we expand the promise of democracy in the face of an unleashed industrialism that gives birth to technocracy and its well-padded production of threats?

Notes

1. Translator's note: Countess von Dönhoff is coeditor of the influential Hamburg weekly *Die Zeit.*
2. Ulrich Rödel, Günter Frankenberg, and Helmut Dubiel, *Die demokratische Frage* (Frankfurt a.M., 1989).

Index

Accountability, 5–6; and incalculability of consequences, 23–24; social-science-based redirection of, 16–17
Adorno, Theodor, 54, 77, 112, 113
Advertising, 67
Ambiguity: of science, 51; unambiguity of science, 90
Anders, Gunther, 25
Arendt, Hannah, 30, 93, 137, 151
Art: knowledge claims of, 90–91
Authority relations, 68
Automation, 58–59
Autonomization: and discontent with modernity, 38–39
Autonomy: institutions deprived of basis of, 143; of science and technology, 102–3; of social systems, 138

Barbarism: enlightenment and, 112; modernization or, 58–59; science as, 98
Beck-Gernsheim, Elisabeth, 99
Bell, Daniel, 113
Benjamin, Walter, 77
Boomerang effect: globalization and, 60
Brecht, Bertolt, 89, 135
Buhl, Walter, 120
Bureaucracy, 137–38
Burgess, John, 121

Causality: ambiguous nature of, 7; and recognition and attribution of hazards, 23–24; and symbolic environmental policy, 10–11
Chernobyl, 91; families affected by, 69–70; information policy, 71; relation to reality transformed by,

65–66; shock interpreted in limited fashion, 69
Christian Democratic Union (Germany), 1
Civil rights: ecology issue as, 8
Class, 135; globalization and boomerang effect and, 60; Marxist theory, 112; pollution and, 59–60
Class formation: individualization and, 40–41
Class struggle, 48; "class struggle without classes" concept, 59; positives at stake in, 3, 122
Comte, Auguste, 77
Conflict scenarios, 26–30
Cubism, 90
Cultural modernization, 39–40
Cultural narcissism: enlightenment vs., 55–58
Culture: ecological protest and symbols of, 124–25; symbols within, 14–15
Cynicism, 82–83

Dahrendorf, Ralf, 59
Danger: Chernobyl transforming awareness of reality of, 65–66; as normal state of affairs, 61
Decision making: risks' origins in, 20
Democracy, 147–51; challenges in risk society to, 70–71; science and, 105–6
Devastation: protest and toleration of, 124
Dialectic of enlightenment, 54–55
Dioxin, 11
Disciplinary society concept, 113
Durkheim, Emile, 114

Ecological conflict: as accountability

153